ADVANCED
READING
INSTRUCTION
IN MIDDLE SCHOOL

GRADES 6–8

ADVANCED
READING
INSTRUCTION
IN MIDDLE SCHOOL
A Novel Approach

Janice I. Robbins, Ph.D.

PRUFROCK PRESS INC.
WACO, TEXAS

Prufrock Press Inc.
P.O. Box 8813
Waco, TX 76714-8813
Phone: (800) 998-2208
Fax: (800) 240-0333
http://www.prufrock.com

Table of Contents

Acknowledgments

With great appreciation to my editor, Lacy Compton, whose expertise has made this book far more than it would otherwise have been. Thanks, also, to the hundreds of my former students, young and not-so-young, who journeyed along with me as we made learning more meaningful through the Novel Approach.

Special thanks to Alicia Bede, an advanced academics resource teacher in Fairfax County, VA, who willingly shared her expertise and classroom experiences in contributing to the chapter on using technology with the Novel Approach.

Dedication

To my favorite reading group and special assistants, my grandchildren: Sydney, Carly, Sophia, Kaitlyn, Melanie, and Austin. They keep me current in the ways of young readers, sharing their favorite books, their reading devices, and their absolute devotion to their favorite genres. They inspire me every day to make school a more exciting place for every reader and every aspiring author.

Overview

If you want to raise the level of student engagement in your reading program, this book is for you. If you want to challenge your advanced students and offer them some new ways of thinking while improving reading comprehension, this book is for you. If you want book recommendations for not-yet-so-mature students who are able to read at an adult level, this book is for you.

Introducing the novel discussion circle as a focus, this book provides a structured process for getting advanced readers in middle grades involved in:

+ reading a variety of novel genres,
+ analyzing the elements of a novel,
+ understanding the author's craft,
+ conceptualizing and using words and phrases purposefully,
+ expanding vocabularies,
+ developing and responding to thought-provoking questions,
+ learning and using effective discussion skills,
+ actively engaging in critical and creative thinking, and
+ identifying and reflecting on general themes and universal ideas.

Sections of the book offer the teacher guidance in:

+ selecting appropriate novels;
+ teaching students to prepare for novel discussions, including:
    - vocabulary and concepts,
    - questioning, and
    - discussing;

+ engaging students in discussion circles, including:
    - preparation,
    - classroom setting,
    - the art of discussion,
    - reflections, and
    - assessments; and

+ directing learning activities to promote cognitive and affective growth.

The book provides information and instructional materials for multiple novel genres including realistic fiction, historical fiction, science fiction, fantasy, mystery, and graphic novels. A section on developmental bibliotherapy suggests the use of novels in support of the unique social and emotional needs of advanced learners. Finally, a section on technology offers ideas for incorporating electronic resources into your Novel Approach to reading.

Chapter 1

Introduction to the Novel Approach

Fiction is the lie that illuminates a greater truth.—Kevin Fox

Reading a good novel is like entering a fictional world where the familiar intersects with the unfamiliar, where what characters think and feel becomes part of your own thinking. Reading a good novel lets you live inside the lives of others while reflecting on your own life in new ways. The "greater truth" that comes from the reading of a novel is your own "greater truth."

This book is about reading novels in the classroom. Specifically, it is written for you, a middle grades teacher, supporting your reading instructional program for advanced students, helping them to find their own "greater truths." In the process, you will teach them to become better at thinking independently, developing confidence in their own reasoning abilities, and transferring insights to new contexts. As presented in this book, the process of advanced reading is one that supports inferential comprehension, language complexity, vocabulary precision, critical listening, and collaborative, reasoned discussion. In this book, you will find purposeful and practical ideas for supporting instruction in each of these areas.

Of course, the first criteria for improving reading skills in advanced readers is to select books that are engaging, rich in figurative language and complexity, present characters who are relatable to young adolescents, and offer intriguing plots and important themes. Advanced adolescent readers are a challenging bunch. Often able to conceptualize at the adult level and comfortable with complex ideas, they nevertheless have limited life experiences. Their social and emotional maturity levels are a mismatch for their cognitive abilities. Selecting good reads can be quite a challenge for you as their teacher, for parents, and for the students themselves. You will find more details about the specific nature and needs of your gifted learners in Chapter 2.

This book includes suggestions for specific novels in multiple genres including realistic fiction, historical fiction, science fiction, fantasy, mystery, and graphic novels. Each novel has been chosen for its complex storylines, richness of language, and highly interesting content. Each will offer you much content for critical and creative thinking and thoughtful discussion. You will also find guidelines for choosing additional novels suitable for advanced middle grades readers. You will discover that the reading, discussion, personal engagement, and reflection activities included in this book can be used with any novel you select for your students.

Getting advanced readers to pick up a book is easy. The challenge for you as the teacher is in getting them to become thoughtful about what they read, how they read it, and how they share the messages they receive from the reading. This reading can occur at three levels: the first between the reader and what is read, the second between the reader and responses to the reading, and the third between the reader and others who have read and reacted to the same book. You will find the Novel Approach a particularly effective method for engaging your gifted learners in all three levels of interaction with novels: reading for enjoyment, digging deeper in completing personal responses to their reading, and, finally, preparing for and participating in a meaningful discussion about the reading. The discussion circle, a regularly scheduled gathering of the small group of students reading the same novel, is the key element in the Novel Approach. It offers students an opportunity to synthesize their understanding of the novel and its underlying meaning and messages in a seminar-like setting.

To support your use of the Novel Approach, this book provides ideas for:
+ engaging advanced learners in reading specific genres,
+ guiding student preparation for novel circle discussions,
+ supporting vocabulary and concept development,
+ activities to strengthen reading comprehension,
+ activities to support critical and creative thinking, and
+ assessment of student learning.

In other sections of the book, you will also find:
+ annotated lists of novels of appropriate interest and complexity for advanced readers in specific genres,
+ instructional guides for understanding general elements of a novel,
+ specific details about each novel genre,
+ use of developmental bibliotherapy in support of advanced learners, and
+ possibilities for blending reading with technology.

I hope your reading journeys and those of your students will be fruitful and enjoyable. May the "greater truths" found in each novel both interest and support new learning for your advanced students.

GETTING STARTED

The following section will offer you a preview of the Novel Approach, including the prescribed process and the responsibilities for you as the teacher as well as those of your students. Figure 1 details the total framework for the Novel Approach.

Prior Learning Related to Questioning and Discussion

Some preparation work is needed to ensure your students will be successful in using the Novel Approach. Students need two skill sets for effective participation in novel discussion groups. First, they must be able to recognize, respond to, and develop open-ended questions, and second, they must be able to share their responses in a way that encourages conversation rather than recitation. This may be a tall order for many students. They are quite familiar with classroom questioning. In general, it is directed and developed by the teacher with the expectation of appropriate responses from students as they are called up to respond. Did you know that research shows that teachers ask about 300–400 questions a day in the classroom? Sixty percent of the questions teachers ask are closed, lower level questions and 20% are procedural, management-type questions. The remaining 20% of questions typically asked are the golden ones, those seeking complex thinking (Cotton, 1995).

Questions asked by students are generally those where they are seeking information or clarification from the teacher. So learning to engage in thoughtful questioning as a lead-in to intellectual discussions is probably new territory for most students. If your students are lucky enough to already have multiple experiences with forming and responding to open-ended questions, you should congratulate yourself and carry on.

Chapter 3 provides suggested activities to engage students in learning how to form thoughtful questions and respond to them. Practice in thoughtful questioning should be completed prior to beginning the novel discussion circles.

Classroom discussions, like most classroom questioning, are completed under the direction of the teacher. The pattern of talk is most often question/answer/comment or asking students to take turns sharing what they know/think/feel. Much raising of hands is evident. These exchanges are not the type of discussion that should occur in the novel discussion circles. Think conversation. In a good conversation, the topic is of interest to the group. Everyone is a participant and, rather than taking turns or raising hands, the participants listen, engage, and connect their comments to those of others in the group. This is the pattern sought for optimum novel discussion groups. It is not easy, because classroom patterns are well established. This type of collaborative discussion is another seldom used instructional medium in the classroom. Teaching students effective discussion skills is essential to success with novel discussion groups. Such skills should be taught prior to engaging students in

	Teacher	Students
Prior Learning	+ Introduce effective questioning + Introduce effective discussions + Teach elements of a novel	+ Participate in lessons + Practice developing questions
Preparation	+ Select appropriate novel + Read the novel + Prepare discussion questions + Form student groups + Provide group schedule + Assign readings, questions, and learning activities + Introduce record keeping	+ Read assigned sections + Complete vocabulary notes + Prepare responses to questions + Prepare optional questions + Maintain records + Complete learning activities
Novel Discussions	+ Facilitate discussion groups + Observe, encourage discussion + Solve problems as needed	+ Prepare for discussion + Interact with discussion group + Share thoughts, ideas, and feelings + Help others to share + Accept group leadership when asked
Activities in Response to Reading	+ Select response activities for completion and sharing	+ Complete assigned responses to reading
Assessment	+ Establish criteria for assessment related to student preparations, discussions, and reading responses + Facilitate assessments	+ Critique personal and group work according to preset criteria for preparation, discussion, and reading responses

Figure 1. The Novel Approach framework and responsibilities.

the actual novel discussion groups. Chapter 4 provides you with multiple ideas for guiding students and practicing thoughtful discussions in small groups.

Preparation for Novel Circle Discussion

You probably get your best teaching ideas from other teachers. Getting students prepared for novel discussion groups can be quite challenging, but if you use the methods found in this book that have been proven to be successful in many class-rooms, then you can be quite sure they will work for you.

Choosing the novel. The first order of business is selecting appropriate novels. What makes a great novel for a typical class of middle grade students may not be the best criteria for your group of advanced readers. These students have unique needs that make novel selection just a bit more challenging. A wide use of figurative language should be present. Rich language should be thought provoking. The plot should be complex and unique. The story may present a paradox, the ending may be nonexistent, or the setting may be rich in fantasy and timelessness.

You may want to select novels connected to the content of your curriculum, such as a particular time period, location, subject, or theme. Alternatively, you may want to focus on realistic novels, highlighting typical issues of middle school students, or you may choose to select novels for a focus on the author's craft or some other novel element like characterization or setting. Whatever your goal, the novel selected should have a special depth of language, complexity of plot, universality of theme, and variance of style so that the students are forced to think about what is being presented both at a surface level and in a more symbolic sense.

The novel selection should address the readability level of the book as well as the maturity level of the students. It is sometimes difficult to match the two and find material that remains within the realm of the child's maturity and yet offers sufficient challenge. Good professional judgment is essential. To help guide you, Chapter 2 contains specific information about the nature and needs of advanced (gifted) readers. To offer you ready-to-use ideas for novels, each chapter on a specific genre (Chapters 7–12) provides annotated lists of suggested books. With a clear understanding of the types of novels required, as well as some readily available suggestions, you are on your way.

Note that when you are making selections of novels, you might want to consider two or three from which a student group may choose to increase motivation for the reading. You will also need to keep in mind that each student needs a copy of the same edition of the novel selected. Because students will be citing pages/paragraphs for sharing what they have found in the novel in response to questions, you want to be sure they are all on the same page!

Once you have your selection made, *you must read the novel.* Do not rely on reviews, synopses, or commentary from others who have read the book. You will do your best teaching when you have experienced the thoughts, ideas, and feelings that you encounter while reading the author's work. This is important. In fact, as you read the novel, record your own ideas in response to the questions you have selected or developed for the novel, just as the students will do. Once you have used a novel in your classroom, you are then ready to reuse that book with future groups. The preparation you do at the beginning will be well worth it. And besides, you will likely enjoy just about all of the recommended books.

Forming questions. You will likely divide the selected novel into reading sections. Develop two or three good, open-ended questions for each section of the book. Questions should be broad enough to allow for a range of thoughts and opinions. Opportunities for students to express their feelings should be incorporated into the questions and related discussion. You will find guidance on developing good questions and helping students to form their own questions in Chapter 3.

Student discussion groups. Student groups should consist of no less than four and no more than eight students. The students selected for a particular group should be fairly close in ability and achievement in reading. If you are using the Novel Approach in a heterogeneous classroom, you may select several novels of the same genre, thus allowing appropriate readability levels for all students while enabling broader class discussion of the story elements in a particular genre of novels. This allows all students to actively participate. If your students are well prepared for the selection, then you may have multiple groups reading and discussing the same novel. If this is your first time with novel discussion groups, do not have more than two different books being discussed at the same time and, ideally, only one author or topic or theme so that the entire class can have follow-up discussions comparing their novels. Specific guidelines for how to conduct novel discussion circles are offered in Chapter 4.

Planning for the novel circle discussion. You may want to consider the length of time for a novel in relation to your grading periods and weekly schedules. Six weeks seems to work quite well from the perspective of student motivation. For a 6-week schedule, you would divide the novel into six parts, assigning one part each week (see Figure 2). This allows sufficient time for student reading to begin in class and continue at home. Depending on the novel, the number of pages for each part may not be equal, considering the total length of the book and the number of pages in each chapter. Be sure that the first section enables students to get well into the characters and the plot of the story.

Scheduling student group work. Provide a schedule for the reading, discussion, and follow-up work. Meeting on a weekly basis puts students into a rhythm that helps them to learn how much time they must allot for reading, for vocabulary and question response preparation, and for any response activities you assign. You may stagger groups so that a different discussion group meets each day. This allows you to monitor discussions and facilitate as needed. Be sure to assign questions, selected response activities of your choice (many of which are available throughout this book), and record-keeping practices. If you have your students 5 days a week, you might consider cycling groups through this schedule:

+ **Day 1:** Assign section reading and questions from the novel. Allow some reading time. Students read and complete vocabulary note taking.
+ **Day 2:** Students continue reading and preparation for discussion. Assign one optional activity related to story elements or genre type.

Week	Pages	Questions	Vocabulary	Elements	Genre	Activities	Assessment

Optional Activity Pages

Week							
1							
2							
3							
4							
5							
6							

Figure 2. Novel discussion group 6-week plan.

+ **Day 3:** Conduct reading discussion group.
+ **Day 4:** Complete reflections and assessment on discussion and share optional activity work.
+ **Day 5:** Assign additional skill building and response activities as well as next reading section.

Note that different groups may begin the cycle on different days of the week if you choose. In this way you will be able to monitor small discussion groups more easily. A sample group schedule is provided in Figure 3.

Getting students ready. Once you have chosen the novel, formed questions, and prepared your schedule for the novel, you are ready to prepare the students. You should present a general overview of the Novel Approach to the group. This can be a whole-class activity if all of the students will be participating in novel circles.

Assessment. Although teacher assessments of student are very personal, the Novel Approach does present great expectations for student involvement in the assessment process. Grading of student progress should certainly take student group and personal assessments into account. Learning activities will become more meaningful as students select their own guidelines for discussion and participation, as well as their personal and group goals for improvement. The development of class, group, and individual assessment tools is encouraged. Sample forms for assessment are included. All of the worksheets should be regarded as examples of specific guides and assignments to help you and your students get organized and well-prepared for each novel discussion. You may want to use or modify them as appropriate for your class. For example, you may require your students to complete journal entries reflecting on their individual and group work instead of using the rating sheets.

You are also encouraged to keep a teacher notebook for the novels you teach. Include your selected questions for each section, section and time divisions, learning activity assignments, assessment, and examples of work and discussion points that will serve as a valuable resource when using the same novel with another group in the future.

Sample Week Schedule				
Group 1	Read	Prepare	Discuss	Reflect and Assess	Complete Activities
Group 2	Complete Activities	Read	Prepare	Discuss	Reflect and Assess
Group 3	Reflect and Assess	Complete Activities	Read	Prepare	Discuss
Group 4	Discuss	Reflect and Assess	Complete Activities	Read	Prepare
Group 5	Prepare	Discuss	Reflect and Assess	Complete Activities	Read

Figure 3. Sample group schedule.

About Your Novel Study

Dear Students,

You are about to begin a new way of reading and responding to novels. I think you will really enjoy having a chance to talk about your reading with a small group of other students. This study is different from pleasure reading in that it is programmed by sections for study, discussion, and activity. Because many of your activities are done in a small group, your responsibilities go beyond personal ones. The others in your group will depend on you to do your best and be prepared.

A notebook divided into the following sections will help you to organize your work:

1. **Student responsibilities:** Keep the list of student responsibilities handy in your notebook so you can refer to it for each discussion circle.

2. **Vocabulary:** As you read your novel section, underline new or interesting vocabulary words. Each week's activities will include some vocabulary work. Your teacher will select or help you choose several experience activities to complete your requirements for the week's work.

3. **Questions:** Whenever you find a place in the novel that would help you explain your answer to one of the questions, record the page number, paragraph (first, second, etc.), key words (the first two words of the paragraph), and a brief comment that will remind you of what you want to say in response to that particular question.

4. **Assessments:** Each week, record your assessment of your participation in the discussion circle. Think about how you can improve or help the group do better.

5. **Learning activities:** You will have different learning activities each week as assigned. Some may be kept in the notebook while others will not be paper assignments. Each week's work should be placed in the appropriate section. Your teacher will present you with the assignments for each week's reading section.

Your reading notebook will be a great record of your novel reading and, especially, the ideas you share with others. Happy reading!

Novel Discussion Circle Responsibilities

Leader

1. Briefly review the novel to date.
2. Read questions for discussion in turn.
3. Encourage courteous interaction of members.
4. Summarize group's response to each question.
5. Guide group evaluation of discussion period.
6. Select next week's leader.
7. Present brief report to teacher. Include members absent or unprepared, general quality of discussion, name of next week's leader.

Group Members

1. Be prepared for discussion.
2. Back up statements with evidence from reading.
3. Listen attentively.
4. Add to idea presented or indicate agreement or courteous disagreement.
5. Respect the opinions of others.
6. Speak one at a time.
7. Participate in a fair evaluation of the group's work.

Assessing Your Work in the Novel Approach

Dear Students,

At the end of each week's novel work, it is important for you to help assess your group's preparation and discussion, as well as your own contributions. You should also make some judgments about the quality of the other learning activities you complete as directed by your teacher.

The personal assessment sheet should be completed at the conclusion of each novel discussion. You will consider several important factors that make a group discussion effective.

Your group leader of the week will also complete a group assessment sheet at the conclusion of the discussion circle. You will be asked to contribute to the thinking about how well the group performed as a whole and anything that would make the next discussion better for everyone in the group.

These assessments allow you to become fully involved in deciding whether or not you have successfully met the criteria for a good discussion as well as specific areas you believe were strong or weak.

Teacher Preparation Check Sheet

- ❑ Select appropriate novel.

- ❑ Read novel. Underline key concepts and vocabulary words.

- ❑ Divide novel into 6–8 sections. Each section will represent a week's work.

- ❑ Develop three open-ended questions for each section.

- ❑ Prepare work outline sheet for entire novel, choosing appropriate activities.

- ❑ Form student groups (4–8 members).

- ❑ Select assessments.

Notes:

_____

_____

_____

_____

_____

Student Preparation Check Sheet

❑ Read the selection for pleasure. Then reread.

❑ Identify and underline new or interesting words/phrases.

❑ Read to record responses to questions.

❑ Think about how events in this section related to the novel as a whole.

❑ Prepare to discuss events and any hidden or deeper meanings you identify in the novel. Is the author revealing a message?

❑ Complete assigned activities.

❑ Complete assigned assessments.

Notes:

_____

_____

_____

_____

_____

Notebook Section for Question Responses

Date for discussion: _____ Week: _____

Novel: _____ Pages: _____

Questions

1. _____

2. _____

3. _____

Question Responses Format

Page	Paragraph	Question #	Key Words	Comments

Notebook Section
Assessment of Personal Contributions to Novel Discussion

MY PERSONAL ASSESSMENT

Date: _____

Novel: _____ Pages: _____

	1	2	3	4	5
Preparation					
Vocabulary					
Participation					
Courtesy					
Connections					

Notes:

_____

_____

_____

_____

_____

My plan for improvement:

_____

_____

_____

_____

_____

Group Leader Assessment of Discussion Circle

Group Members: _____

_____

Date: _____

Novel: _____ Pages: _____

	1	2	3	4	5
Preparation					
Vocabulary					
Participation					
Courtesy					
Connections					

Notes:

_____

_____

_____

_____

_____

Our areas for improvement:

_____

_____

_____

_____

17

Chapter 2

The Gifted Reader

So Matilda's strong young mind continued to grow, nurtured by the voices of all of those authors who had sent their books out into the world like ships on the sea. These books gave Matilda a comforting message: You are not alone.—Roald Dahl, *Matilda*

Did you ever find yourself asking a child to put her half-hidden library book away and pay attention? One of the most revealing traits of giftedness you are likely to notice in students is their voracious appetite for reading. And these highly able, verbally precocious readers may be performing at a typical age level in other content areas and may not require curricular changes in other subjects. Gifted students are a diverse group, so for the purposes of this book we are addressing the needs of students who are advanced in reading and those who require more challenging instructional activities in reading, changes that are more than a simple acceleration of their reading level.

Advanced readers spend many more hours reading each week than their age peers. Of course, not all of your gifted students are avid readers, but most are. Many may lose motivation for typical classroom reading activities because of their ability to read more quickly and at higher levels. Most of their reading occurs outside of the classroom. These students need different challenges beyond those available from conventional reading instruction.

Many advanced students also have extensive vocabularies and deep conceptual understanding. They are capable of reading texts two or, quite often, many years beyond their grade level. These advanced capabilities require you to consider the careful selection of literature and related learning activities. Your students have acquired decoding skills and basic comprehension skills and, likely, a good facility with words. Instructional experiences you provide should direct them to broader and deeper understanding and emotional connections with the author's message.

You may recognize advanced readers by looking for these traits:

+ early readers, often independent of instruction;
+ performance in reading significantly above grade level;
+ real enjoyment of reading;
+ extensive reading;
+ demonstrated "need to read" in response to personal quest for information;
+ strong focus on reading tasks;
+ creative interpretations of the story;
+ strong emotional connections to story elements;
+ motivation to act upon ideas gained from reading; and
+ desire for variety in reading genres.

Although many gifted readers choose from a variety of reading genres, this is not always the case. Boys in general spend less time reading than girls and tend to choose informational and special interest texts, while girls gravitate toward narrative stories. Both genders of this age seem to have a particular affinity for novels in a series and, for advanced readers in particular, fantasy or science fiction series. When given the impetus to expand their reading selections, students stuck in a particular genre begin to gravitate to a wider variety of genres, learning to appreciate the intricacies of each type of novel.

Your advanced readers are ready for experiences that open their minds, extend their curiosity, and encourage their connection to the characters they meet and the author's message. Through the reading and discussion of novels your advanced students can learn to:

+ look beyond the obvious;
+ expand their vocabularies;
+ interpret nuanced, complex language;
+ extend conceptual knowledge;
+ manipulate complex ideas;
+ relate to characters and situations;
+ articulate and appreciate abstract ideas;
+ gain deeper understanding of the text; and
+ expand their imaginative interpretations.

Table 1 addresses the particular characteristics of advanced readers, corresponding instructional outcomes, and the strategies and content contained in the Novel Approach that make it particularly effective for advanced readers. As you begin to use the instructional strategies outlined in the remaining chapters of this book, you will recognize the significance of each of the components in the Novel Approach. You will also recognize the growth of your students as they individually and collectively approach each reading with curious anticipation, extensive analysis

Table 1

Gifted Readers and the Novel Approach

Gifted Readers' Characteristics	Appropriate and Challenging Student Outcomes	Strategies in Novel Approach
Achievement above grade level.	Read assigned and self-selected texts of advanced depth and complexity.	Use of selected high-interest, intellectually challenging books with appropriate maturity level.
Great enjoyment of reading.	Collaborate with intellectual peers to deepen and extend understanding and appreciation of author's message.	Defined processes to support collaborative exploration, analysis, and synthesis of new ideas.
Extensive, often voracious reading.	Explore a variety of issues and ideas. Explore and use new words, language, and broad concepts.	Varied universal themes analyzed through reading reflection activities. Extended use of concept development and vocabulary activities.
Curiosity and intense quest for new knowledge.	Develop and respond to questions seeking new and expanded information.	Development of student question-asking skills and use of open-ended questions for discussions.
Ability to remain focused on thoughtful reading tasks.	Develop personal reading strategies for critical and creative thinking.	Direct teaching of critical and creative thinking strategies.
Creative interpretations.	Develop creative thinking skills, expanded imagery, and imaginative interpretations.	Selected individual reflection and group interactive activities in support of creative imagery and interpretations.
Emotional connections.	Express feelings and empathetic connections to book characters and real-life parallels. Learn different ways of looking at themselves and others.	Group dialogue connecting novel elements to individual and group feelings. Guidance on use of developmental bibliotherapy.
Reading of a variety of genres.	Demonstrate understanding of elements of different novel genres and related author's craft for each genre.	Lessons for developing understanding of author's purposeful use of novel elements in each genre.

of the story's elements, and interpretive conclusions that make each reading both a personal journey and a reflection of the universality of the story.

When you use the Novel Approach as a regular part of your instruction plan, you are providing your advanced learners with a strong component of a total language arts program that uses specific motivational and cognitive development components geared toward increased reading comprehension. Specific comprehension skills include fluency, concept development, assumptions, inferences, and interpretations. These powerful cognitive reading skills are applicable to all forms of reading and all reading content. When you help your students build critical and creative reading skills, you provide them with tools for a lifetime. Helping students learn effective discussion skills also promotes connections, collaboration, and clarity in sharing ideas with others. These important social skills build student confidence and ability to communicate effectively with others.

Guiding Students in Personal Novel Selection and Reading

The Novel Approach is generally used with book selections you have purposefully chosen for your students. You choose books to address your students' readiness, interests, and instructional goals. You can also help your students choose books for their personal reading that expand their familiarity with different genres, different authors, and different levels of complexity. The following guidelines are offered to help you support your students' selections of quality novels beyond those required for classroom reading groups:

1. **Help students to choose carefully!** Hundreds of thousands of books are published each year. Encourage them to develop ways in which they can sift through the many to get to the few books of greatest value to them. You may suggest book reviews or lists of award winners. Encourage them to seek recommendations of friends, teachers, or librarians. Teach them the old adage, "Don't judge a book by its cover." Provide opportunities for students to share books they would recommend to their classmates.

2. **Ask students to get acquainted with different authors.** Knowing the author's background, previous works, and style of writing can help students to predict whether or not a particular book is the right one for them. Some authors write books in a series. Most stay within a particular genre. Encourage them to give multiple authors a chance. You may set up an "Author" blog where students each provide information on a particular author they enjoy.

3. **Encourage variety in reading from different genres.** Some students like variety in their reading, moving from genre to genre and enjoying what each style has to offer. Other readers are stuck in one place, always choosing science fiction or some other type of novel. Ask students to branch out and challenge themselves to learn the merits of all types of writing. You might focus on a particular genre each month, offering students a chance to create a display related to the genre and encouraging small-group book sharing of favorites they have discovered.

4. **Remind students that these are fictional works!** Good fiction writing grabs the reader from the beginning. In a special way the reader enters the world of the characters. Writers of fiction draw from real life, but add their own embellishments to people, places, and events. Good writers make the story seem authentic, but help students to see that while the book may be based on real people and real events, the author has taken literary license to mold the story to his or her personal criteria to make your reading experience top notch. Offer students the opportunity to share real-life stories that might be the basis for good novels.

5. **Ask students to step into the shoes of the main characters.** Most novels revolve around a main character or a small group of characters whose actions and reactions move the plot along. Encourage students to begin a character list

as they start a novel, taking notes of the first characters introduced to determine who the critical players are likely to be. Students are often confused at the start of a novel when several characters are quickly introduced. You may demonstrate how to build a character web or tree that can be expanded as the story unfolds.

6. **Help students to connect the dots.** From the beginning of the story to the end, the reader is traveling on a journey. Help students to follow the unfolding story in a way that works for them. The author often uses each chapter as a way of keeping a focus.

7. **Suggest that students keep a notebook handy.** Even those who read just for pleasure often keep a notepad for jotting thoughts and ideas. Help students to recognize reading as a personal adventure and one that is more enjoyable when they are active readers. Suggest that some readers like to tab pages or write in the margins or underline particularly interesting phrases, beautiful language, or unknown terms to enhance their reading experiences.

8. **Guide students to look for the "big picture."** Authors have a purpose in mind when they develop a novel. It is often a "lesson" or some theme that is important to them, like "all humans must work together for the protection of our planet," or "true friendship requires selfless acts."

9. **Help students to relish words and phrases.** Remember that little notebook? It is also a great place to record unusual words or phrases students meet in their reading. Encourage them to write down particularly interesting phrases, beautiful language, or unknown terms.

10. **Encourage students to share their thoughts.** One of the great things about reading a good book is seeing if others also enjoyed it. People have different tastes and experiences and something one person reads may be an all-time favorite for him or her, but may not spark the same reaction in others. Asking students to share recommendations with their peers is a great way to extend the reading selections of your students.

11. **Teach students to rate their reading experiences.** The end of a book is a good time to do a little personal reflecting. Ask students to keep a journal where they comment about the books they have read. Let them know that they may find the journal helpful as a record. Perhaps they will want to read something by the same author, or they might want to avoid that author in the future. Perhaps they will read another novel of the same genre. They will likely have several great recommendations for friends and family looking for a good book to read. Encourage students to write a formal review to be submitted to an online group that reviews novels. In this way you are encouraging them to connect with the reading public, sharing their points of view with many people.

The Gifted Reader's Bill of Rights

+ The right to read at a pace and level appropriate to readiness without regard to grade placement.
+ The right to discuss interpretations, issues, and insights with intellectual peers.
+ The right to reread many books and not finish every book.
+ The right to use reading to explore new and challenging information and grow intellectually.
+ The right for time to pursue a self-selected topic in depth through reading and writing.
+ The right to encounter and apply increasingly advanced vocabulary, word study, and concepts.
+ The right to guidance rather than dictation of what is good literature and how to find the best.
+ The right to read several books at the same time.
+ The right to discuss but not have to defend reading choice and taste.
+ The right to be excused from material already learned.

Note. From *Differentiation: Simplified, realistic, and effective* (p. 189) by B. L. Kingore, 2004, Austin, TX: Professional Associates. Reprinted with permission.

Chapter 3

The Art of Questioning

All our knowledge results from questions, which is another way of saying that question-asking is our most important intellectual tool.—Neil Postman

You want your students' novel group discussions to be successful. You have selected a novel that will appeal to most of your students and now you are ready to assign sections of the novel in preparation for the discussions. After the selection of the novel, the next most important thing is the questions used in the discussion. These are more important than the answers, because it is in thinking about and responding to the questions that real changes in the students' thinking occur. Questions posed for the reading should provoke deep thought and interpretations of the author's words supported by evidence from the reading. This type of thinking requires careful reading and analysis. Thus, with the right questions, students are engaging in higher level thinking involving analyzing, evaluating, and creating. These three levels of the revised Bloom's taxonomy are keys to critical and creative thinking. Because responses are interpretive, they have the capacity to offer new insight into the author's creativity as much as firmly supported conclusions. This chapter offers guidance and practice in developing higher level questions. Additional student activities begin on page 39.

Questions should *not* be about basic information or those whose answers are right there, specific, and precise. These are called *closed questions*. Once the correct response has been offered, thinking stops. Examples of closed questions include:
+ Who was Ana's best friend?
+ What did Orion have in his left hand?
+ When did Mitchell move to Oregon?
+ Where did the story take place?

But don't be fooled! Just because a question starts with who, what, when, or where, you cannot assume that what follows makes it a closed question. Consider these:

+ Who in this book reminds you of someone you know?
+ What could have made the townspeople run in terror?
+ When did Orion begin to believe that her magic powers were useful?
+ Where were instances in the reading that helped you predict what would happen next?

Often people think that "why" questions are the thought-provoking ones. But consider this example:

+ Why was Mary crying? (Because her dog was lost.)

Is this a closed question? Yes, it is! There is one correct response.

Closed questions are very valuable for finding facts, focusing attention, and checking recall. Closed questions are not helpful in generating discussion and provoking deep and expansive thinking.

So just relying on question stems will not enable you to generate open, thought-provoking questions. Open questions have no right or wrong answers. These questions invite a variety of reasonable responses, are open to interpretation, and allow for multiple responses and points of view. They require thoughtful consideration of what was read. There are no right answers. Here are some examples of open questions:

+ What factors do you think Jason was considering when he had to make the choice between going or staying with the clan?
+ Was Monique a believable character?
+ If this event had happened today, what would be different?
+ How did your perceptions of Bret and Arthur change as you learned more about their actions?
+ What do you predict might happen in the next chapter?
+ What words did the author use to set the mood for this section of the story?

As you can see, each of the open questions asks for some interpretation that requires an analysis of the printed words. Students will be asked to consider what they read, what it meant, what it could mean, and how they reacted to it. The skills of analyzing, evaluating, and creating are incorporated into questions like these. Emotional and imaginative responses are also sought. What will guide you in the development of open questions is your own thinking about potential responses to each question. You are working to develop thought-provoking questions, those that may have a number of possible responses as opposed to one correct answer. A good test of the value of your question for group discussion is whether or not you can come up with at least three different possibilities for your response. Questions like this are generating thought and that is what you are seeking.

As you learn more about the strategies used in the novel discussion groups, you will recognize the extreme importance of the questions asked. They are the guides to thinking. For now, it is most important that you become comfortable with developing effective open-ended questions. The activities included in this chapter will guide you and your students through the process so that you become comfortable with understanding the types of questions (open and closed) and the variety of questions (thinking, feeling, and imagining) that should be asked.

Teaching your students to generate these thought-provoking questions has two benefits. First, they will come to understand the difference between gaining information that is readily available and thinking analytically about something and coming to conclusions that required real thinking. Second, as your students become proficient at asking thoughtful questions, they will become the generators of questions for the novel discussion groups. You will find that they get pretty good at this and are able to generate questions you would never have considered.

So how do you teach students effective questioning? The revised Bloom's taxonomy (Anderson & Krathwohl, 2001) is a good tool, but be sure you guide students to recognize the difference between higher order, open questions and lower order, closed questions.

Figure 4 offers a view of verbs related to each of the levels of Bloom's taxonomy. You may use this chart to help students recognize the differences across the levels, but remember that a good question requires more than a particular verb. The test of a truly open questions is, "Does this question require responses that cannot be found directly in the reading? Does this question require an analysis and interpretation of what was read or a reimagining of the idea?"

The following generic questions may help you as you begin your question development for each novel. Remember that the best questions will be the ones you develop to match your students, your personal reading of the book, and the areas of emphasis you choose for instruction. Use the Bloom's taxonomy chart and these question starters as a guide to stimulate your own thinking and that of your students.

Question Starters for Novels

Analyzing Questions
+ Why do you think the author chose this title?
+ Can you find two examples of (emotion) in this section?
+ Compare (character) and (character). Which one is (stronger, more likeable, more like you)?
+ Which character is showing the greatest need for support?

Focus for Closed, Lower Order Questioning		
Remembering	**Understanding**	**Applying**
list	describe	use
name	explain	apply
recall	summarize	carry out
Focus for Open, Higher Order Questioning		
Analyzing	**Evaluating**	**Creating**
compare	criticize	design
deconstruct	evaluate	combine
infer	decide	produce
connect	defend	rewrite
conclude	rank	role play
illustrate	score	reorganize
prioritize	critique	express
differentiate	debate	invent
assume	distinguish	produce
interpret	justify	compose
cite	persuade	anticipate

Figure 4. Bloom's taxonomy in action.

+ In what ways has the author helped you to visualize the setting of this story?
+ What is the connection between this section and what happened in the last section?
+ Can you compare the problem our protagonist is facing with a problem you have experienced?
+ What choices does the protagonist face? The antagonist?
+ How do the characters interact with each other?
+ What is the tone of the writing in this section?

Evaluating Questions
+ What was the author trying to accomplish in this part of the book? Did he or she accomplish this?
+ What is your opinion of (character) now? What evidence do you have to support your opinion?
+ What makes this book believable or unbelievable? Does that impact your judgment of the book?
+ Can you picture what is happening? Is the author's use of imagery weak, adequate, or strong? Why do you say that?
+ What is this author's greatest strength?
+ Who do you think is the real hero in this story?
+ What are some possible themes for this book?
+ Which character is the most likeable? Why?
+ Should this story have a happy ending?
+ Should this novel be on the Top Ten List for students in your school?
+ Write a negative (positive) book review for this novel.

Creating/Synthesizing Questions
+ Write a four-line poem about this section of the book.
+ What if (character) were older/richer/different gender/more powerful? What might happen?
+ Can you anticipate the ending of the story at this point in your reading?
+ What scene from this book would make a good one-act play?
+ If you changed the personality of one character, whose would it be? Why?
+ Find a section from the reading to prepare a dramatic reading with a partner.
+ What if (character's) superpower were combined with the ability to read minds?
+ Develop an alternative list of titles for this novel.
+ Can you develop a storyline for a sequel to this novel?
+ What if you changed one event in this section? What would it be and how would it alter the plot?

+ Write a journal entry one of the characters in this section might have written.

The most important learning for your students is to be able to recognize and develop questions that spark discussion, the open-ended type. Recognize that this is likely new territory for you and your students, so take the time to ensure conceptual understanding of the difference between the lower level and higher level questions. Because these higher level questions will require critical and creative thinking, you do not need to assign more than two or three questions per session.

The learning activity pages that follow will help you to introduce questioning to your students and promote an environment in which novel reading promotes powerful questioning and stimulating discussions.

Practice Lesson
The Art and Practice of Good Questioning

As students read and prepare for the discussion group, they should be taught the importance of the question and the ways in which different types of questions call for different types of responses. The following lesson is a good start.

Objective

Prepare students for responding to and developing open-ended questions to guide novel circle discussions.

Lesson at a Glance

+ Students uncover the difference between closed and open questions.
+ Students learn about Bloom's taxonomy as a guide to effective questioning.
+ Students practice developing open-ended questions.
+ Students practice locating reading passages that support responses to higher level questions.

Instructions

1. Help your students to determine the difference between open and closed questions. Display the following as a chart:

    Open or Closed Questions:
    a. Who is the author of this novel?
    b. Describe Kyle's appearance.
    c. What images come to your mind when you hear the title?
    d. Compare the personalities of the first two characters you meet in the novel.
    e. When was this book published?
    f. How does the hero express his interest in making the town a better place?

    Tell students that some questions are open and some are closed. Ask for volunteers to suggest the difference and summarize by developing a brief statement about open and closed questions, recording it for display. Be sure they understand and articulate that closed questions are those with only one correct response and than open questions allow for multiple responses.

CHAPTER 3 Materials

2. Tell students that they will now practice their understanding of open and closed questions. Distribute the "I Pity Them" handout. Ask students to read and, as they read, develop three questions that could be answered by other students who might read this text in the future. Let them know that any questions are appropriate. They do not have to think about whether they are open or closed at this point.

3. When students have completed their reading and question development, ask them to work with a partner to think about their questions in terms of types. Is the question "closed," having one correct answer or is it an "open" question, having no particular answer but several possible answers?

4. Ask student partnerships to share one of their questions without labeling them open or closed. After the students read the question a second time, ask the class whether the question should be added to a chart labeled **Open** or a chart labeled **Closed**. Record each question on the appropriate chart, numbering questions as you add them to each chart.

5. Next, ask student partnerships to select one question from the closed question list and one question from the open question list. Once they have identified their questions, ask them to locate places in the reading that help them to answer each question and label them in the handout with the question number.

6. Guide a brief discussion, asking students to select a question, provide a response, and then tell where they found text to support their response. Encourage others to respond to the same question, also citing text locations. Suggest that students use the paragraph numbers as helpful in citing the location of the evidence in the reading. Continue the sharing and be sure students recognize whether the question was open or closed, having one specific response or several possibilities for thinking through a response. This discussion teaches students how to look for passages that help them to respond to the questions for each reading section. Their preparation for the discussion is dependent upon their ability to analyze the text for evidence that supports their thinking about responses to questions.

7. Distribute copies of the Bloom's taxonomy verb list in Figure 4 and introduce this to students as a good guide to effective questioning. Also distribute the second reading passage, an excerpt from *The Adventures of Huckleberry Finn* by Mark Twain. Ask them to consider which of the levels of this taxonomy are likely to offer the most open-ended questions and why. Ask them to practice using the taxonomy with their partner to develop one question for each of the higher level verbs (analyzing, evaluating, creating), using the passage from *The Adventures of Huckleberry Finn*.

8. Ask students to share their questions and help the class to distinguish among the levels by having them guess which level each question supports. Reconcile differences of opinion and let students know that the categorization is less important than the idea that each question should make them think broadly and deeply.

9. Briefly discuss the use of the taxonomy and explain that they should keep this handout, as they will find it helpful in the future as they participate in the Novel Approach. Let them know that you will be using it to develop questions for them to use with their readings and that they will also be asked to develop one good open-ended question to bring to each discussion circle.

10. Ask students to reflect on the importance of open-ended questions and record a personal statement about their value. Locate a space for students to display their statements (chart, bulletin board, class blog, etc.) for future inspiration.

"I Pity Them"

Paragraph

1 A poor man once undertook to emigrate from Castine, Me., to Illinois. When he was attempting to cross a river in New York, his horse broke through the rotten timbers of the bridge, and was drowned. He had but this one animal to convey all his property and his family to his new home.

2 His wife and children were almost miraculously saved from sharing the fate of the horse; but the loss of this poor animal was enough. By its aid the family, it may be said, had lived and moved; now they were left helpless in a land of strangers, without the ability to go on or return, without money or a single friend to whom to appeal. The case was a hard one.

3 There were a great many who "passed by on the other side." Some even laughed at the predicament in which the man was placed; but by degrees a group of people began to collect, all of whom pitied him.

4 Some pitied him a great deal, and some did not pity him very much, because, they said he might have known better than to try to cross an unsafe bridge, and should have made his horse swim the river. Pity, however, seemed rather to predominate. Some pitied the man, and some the horse; all pitied the poor, sick mother and her six helpless children.

5 Among this pitying party was a rough son of the West, who knew what it was like to migrate some hundreds of miles over new roads to locate a destitute family on a prairie. Seeing the man's forlorn situation, and looking around on the bystanders, he said, "All of you seem to pity these poor people very much, but I would beg leave to ask each of you how much."

6 "There, stranger," continued he, holding up a ten-dollar bill, "there is the amount of my pity; and if others will do as I do, you may soon get another pony. God bless you." It is needless to state the effect that this active charity produced. In a short time the happy emigrant arrived at his destination, and he is now a thriving farmer, and a neighbor to him who was his "friend in need, and a friend indeed."

Note. From *McGuffy's Fifth Eclectic Reader* (pp. 85–86), 1879, New York, NY: American Book Company.

The Adventures of Huckleberry Finn

by Mark Twain (Samuel Clemens)

Chapter 1
Paragraph

1 YOU don't know about me without you have read a book by the name of The Adventures of Tom Sawyer; but that ain't no matter. That book was made by Mr. Mark Twain, and he told the truth, mainly. There was things which he stretched, but mainly he told the truth. That is nothing.

2 I never seen anybody but lied one time or another, without it was Aunt Polly, or the widow, or maybe Mary. Aunt Polly—Tom's Aunt Polly, she is—and Mary, and the Widow Douglas is all told about in that book, which is mostly a true book, with some stretchers, as I said before.

    Now the way that the book winds up is this: Tom and me found the money that the robbers hid in the cave, and it made us rich. We got six thousand dollars apiece—all gold. It was an awful sight of money when it was piled up. Well, Judge Thatcher he took it and put it out at interest, and it fetched us a dollar a day apiece all the year round—more than a body could tell what to do with.

3 The Widow Douglas she took me for her son, and allowed she would sivilize me; but it was rough living in the house all the time, considering how dismal regular and decent the widow was in all her ways; and so when I couldn't stand it no longer I lit out. I got into my old rags and my sugar-hogshead again, and was free and satisfied.

4 But Tom Sawyer he hunted me up and said he was going to start a band of robbers, and I might join if I would go back to the widow and be respectable. So I went back. The widow she cried over me, and called me a poor lost lamb, and she called me a lot of other names, too, but she never meant no harm by it. She put me in them new clothes again, and I couldn't do nothing but sweat and sweat, and feel all cramped up.

5 Well, then, the old thing commenced again. The widow rung a bell for supper, and you had to come to time. When you got to the table you couldn't go right to eating, but you had to wait for the widow to tuck down her head and grumble a little over the victuals, though there warn't really anything

the matter with them,—that is, nothing only everything was cooked by itself.

6   In a barrel of odds and ends it is different; things get mixed up, and the juice kind of swaps around, and the things go better. After supper she got out her book and learned me about Moses and the Bulrushers, and I was in a sweat to find out all about him; but by and by she let it out that Moses had been dead a considerable long time; so then I didn't care no more about him, because I don't take no stock in dead people.

7   Pretty soon I wanted to smoke, and asked the widow to let me. But she wouldn't. She said it was a mean practice and wasn't clean, and I must try to not do it any more. That is just the way with some people. They get down on a thing when they don't know nothing about it. Here she was a-bothering about Moses, which was no kin to her, and no use to any-body, being gone, you see, yet finding a power of fault with me for doing a thing that had some good in it. And she took snuff, too; of course that was all right, because she done it herself.

8   Her sister, Miss Watson, a tolerable slim old maid, with gog-gles on, had just come to live with her, and took a set at me now with a spelling-book. She worked me middling hard for about an hour, and then the widow made her ease up. I couldn't stood it much longer. Then for an hour it was deadly dull, and I was fidgety. Miss Watson would say, "Don't put your feet up there, Huckleberry;" and "Don't scrunch up like that, Huckleberry—set up straight;" and pretty soon she would say, "Don't gap and stretch like that, Huckleberry—why don't you try to behave?"

9   Then she told me all about the bad place, and I said I wished I was there. She got mad then, but I didn't mean no harm. All I wanted was to go somewheres; all I wanted was a change, I warn't particular. She said it was wicked to say what I said; said she wouldn't say it for the whole world; she was going to live so as to go to the good place. Well, I couldn't see no advantage in going where she was going, so I made up my mind I wouldn't try for it. But I never said so, because it would only make trouble, and wouldn't do no good.

Name: _____ Date: _____

Remembering

Have you ever played 20 Questions? In this variation, your task is simply to compose 10 questions about this week's section that can be quickly answered "yes" or "no" by others in your group.

Page	Question	Answer

The 10-question task was fairly easy and now you are ready to use your questions on your group. Have a "yes"/"no" session during which all members have chances to ask and answer questions. Following the session, write your reaction to this activity on the lines below.

_____

_____

_____

_____

CHAPTER 3 Materials

Rank the question session on this scale:

	Strongly Disagree			Strongly Agree
1. We learned many new things.	0	- - - - - - - - - - - - - -	- - - - - - - - -	10
2. We thought deeply and intensely.	0	- - - - - - - - - - - - - -	- - - - - - - - -	10
3. We felt stimulated and challenged.	0	- - - - - - - - - - - - - -	- - - - - - - - -	10
4. We showed creativity.	0	- - - - - - - - - - - - - -	- - - - - - - - -	10
5. We found the task dull and boring.	0	- - - - - - - - - - - - - -	- - - - - - - - -	10
6. We were asked to recall information.	0	- - - - - - - - - - - - - -	- - - - - - - - -	10

Your work on questioning was at the Remembering level of thinking.

Forming questions that ask for facts to be recalled is a type of thinking often classified as Remembering. At this level of thought, the learner shows some knowledge of some basics. Questions often start with words such as who, what, when, or where. The learner may be asked to match, list, recall, underline, pick, say, or show.

At the Remembering level, it is easy for us to decide whether an answer is correct or incorrect.

Write five Remembering questions about yourself. Share questions and answers with a partner.

_____

_____

_____

_____

_____

_____

_____

_____

Understanding

Get together with your group and spend some time summarizing one part of the book round-robin style. The first person begins the story and tells a bit about what happened and then allows the next person to continue, and so on.

In this activity, you are functioning at the Understanding level of thinking, showing that you *understand* what you have read. Questions at this level ask the learner to restate something, give an example, illustrate, define, summarize, or otherwise prove that the knowledge or basic facts have been internalized.

Now work in a group to help each other form a set of Understanding-level questions. First, each member of the group should record two or three questions that are probably at this level. Questions should be read aloud and a decision made as to whether or not they fit the understanding mold. After the discussion, place "Y" (yes), "P" (probably yes), or "N" (probably no) beside each of your questions. Following the activity, write your reaction to this type of questioning.

Questions

_____

_____

_____

_____

_____

_____

_____

Reaction

_____

_____

_____

_____

_____

Applying

At the Applying level, you are asked to use your knowledge in some way. The question may ask you to organize your facts, construct a model, draw or paint an example, collect data from the reading, or demonstrate or dramatize an event.

You often apply your knowledge in reading by preparing a poster, a mobile, a new book jacket, a sculpture, a scrapbook, or some tangible item to share your interpretation of the reading.

Think about ways you could apply your understanding of this week's reading section. With your group, form a very large chart of Applying projects for reading.

From the class list, select one application of interest to you and complete it. Share your project with the class.

Personal ideas for Applying projects:

_____

_____

_____

_____

_____

Project I have selected to complete to show the Applying level of thinking:

_____

_____

_____

_____

_____

Reaction

_____

_____

_____

_____

_____

In a few words, tell how the first three levels of thinking are alike and how they differ.

_____

_____

_____

_____

_____

_____

_____

_____

_____

_____

Analyzing

Analyzing asks the learner to examine the facts, to classify, survey, experiment, categorize, or explore. In general, you should look at something in depth at this level. Most of the reading questions your teacher presents for each section are at the Analyzing level.

    Below, list some of the problems (major or minor) faced by characters in your book thus far. You won't find these on a page labeled "problems." This task requires you to examine and to classify what you have read. This is analyzing.

_____

_____

_____

_____

_____

_____

Use some of these "starter" words to help you write four questions about the problems you found in the novel that could be discussed in your reading circle group. Be sure they are at the Analyzing level:

+ take apart
+ analyze
+ categorize

+ compare
+ contrast
+ subdivide

+ classify
+ outline

Work with a partner and analyze each other's work to decide whether or not your questions are at the Analyzing level.

_____

_____

_____

_____

_____

_____

_____

Advanced Reading Instruction in Middle School © Prufrock Press Inc.

Name: _____ Date: _____

Evaluating

Most people think of evaluation in the sense of, "Did I do a good job?" This is certainly one form of evaluating, probably the most familiar. When we consider evaluative thinking, we go beyond wondering about somebody's opinion of us and our performance.

We become thinkers who judge anything or any person *according to some standard* decided upon beforehand. The setting of standards or criteria is very important so that we have something to compare to the product or idea we hope to judge. Many activities in this book ask you to rank performance, effort, or feelings on a scale; to criticize a character's feelings or actions; to debate the importance of a particular event; or to comment upon the value of a particular activity in your own learning. These are examples of the Evaluating level.

Self-evaluation is the best way to determine how well you are learning. Consider what things are important to know or to practice in order to improve your critical reading ability. Brainstorm ideas with your group and list some here (for example, "Understanding word meanings.").

_____

_____

_____

_____

_____

Select five skills you should definitely possess. Rank your ability in each area in some way.

_____

_____

_____

How will you know if you improve or master the skills you have selected? Think of a way you could evaluate your progress.

_____

_____

_____

Creating

The Creating level of thinking is perhaps the most exciting level of thought. It is at this level that your mind plays around with new information you have received and forms new images and ideas. The knowledge you received combines with what you already have to make a new connection.

Here are some good process and product words for the Creating level:

Process

+ imagine
+ combine
+ role play
+ compose

+ invent
+ predict
+ create
+ design

+ adapt
+ develop

Product

+ game
+ invention
+ show/script
+ song

+ store
+ diagram
+ model
+ product

+ cartoon
+ poem

Mix and match some processes with some products to come up with three Creating activities—one for you, one for a book character, one for a special talent your teacher has—all related in some way to your novel.

Creating Activities

For me:

_____

_____

_____

_____

_____

Creating, Continued

For a character:

_____

_____

_____

_____

_____

For my teacher:

_____

_____

_____

_____

_____

Imagining

Get ready for a mind journey. Relax all of your body parts . . . close your eyes . . . and open your mind's eye. In front of you place a book . . . make it small, about the size of a peanut. Who will read it? Place a reader in front of the book. Now make the book and the reader grow larger and larger . . .

Test out the above mind journey on a friend. Discuss the experience. What can you think of to continue this image? Will the book reader become even larger? Angry? Disappear? Just about anything can happen as you use your imagination.

Training your mind's eye to see things in different ways helps you to become more flexible in your thinking. Authors use this technique to imagine the action, the people, and the setting for their novels.

Now think of something that is flexible (such as a sneaker, a sock, a pancake, a blade of grass) and create a mind journey.

Read it to a friend. Talk about the images formed. How could they get better? Could your writing be improved?

A Flexible Journey

Record your mind journey here:

_____

_____

_____

_____

_____

Comments about your journey:

_____

_____

_____

_____

_____

Name: _____ Date: _____

Imagery Sharing

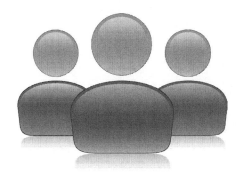

Prepare a mind voyage for your group by selecting a section from your novel to read aloud. As you search for a passage, consider one that appeals to as many senses as possible. After you have chosen your reading, try it out with a partner. Have the other person read it aloud to you as you relax and form clear mind pictures. If you are satisfied with your selection, prepare it for reading to the group. You may want to skip parts of it. Be sure to read clearly, distinctly, and slowly enough for group members to get the picture. Try to recall your own mental images as you read it.

My reading selection:

_____

Vivid words and phrases are:

_____

_____

_____

_____

_____

My selection especially appeals to these senses:

_____

_____

_____

_____

_____

Crazy Imagery

Record any 10 objects in the table below. Beside each add an adjective/noun combination found in this week's reading.

Object	Adjective and Noun

Think about combining the objects and adjective/noun combinations. Form mind pictures. Make them humorous! Write your three funniest images in sentence form.

_____

_____

_____

_____

_____

Name: _____ Date: _____

Graphic Story

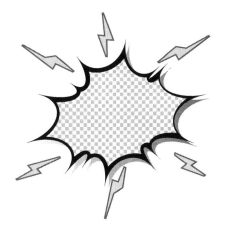

Think about ways you could tell a story without words. How can you share your mind pictures with someone else without writing about them in words? This is the way graphic novelists work to tell a story.

Think about this week's reading section from your novel. What if you could use mainly pictures and very few words to tell about this section of the novel. How would it look? Try a few pictures then share it with a friend. Did they "get" the story? Discuss your results and write a comment about this experience.

_____

_____

_____

_____

_____

What If?

Picture these in your mind.

+ What if all of the characters in your book turned into animals? What would each become?
+ What if someone in the story had a magic nose? Who would it be? What would the nose do?
+ What would happen if everyone grew to be giant-sized or shrunk?
+ What if the main character had an imaginary rabbit friend?
+ What if every green thing turned purple?
+ What if a war started? How would it change the novel?

Get Dramatic

With your group, choose a few pages from this week's section that would be suitable for dramatization. Choose a narrator and select character parts. Practice reading with expression. Tape your dramatic reading and play it back for your evaluation.

Your group may decide to act out the selection with gestures, simple costumes, and props. Each actor should try to "see" the character being portrayed in his or her mind's eye. Imitate facial expressions and body postures and movements suitable for the particular character.

Perform only after several practice sessions to smooth things out. Judge audience reaction to your presentation.

Make a Book Cover

Most novels leave a picture in your mind's eye, but often a publisher asks for a few sketches to accompany the text for the book cover or for advertising purposes.

Think about this week's reading section. Which events or places or people are most vivid in your mind?

Try not to think about them in words, only pictures. Can you see one with all its details?

On a separate piece of paper, do some sketching until you are satisfied with one. Keep referencing back to your mind's picture as you need help.

Chapter 4

Thoughtful Discussion

Discussion is impossible with someone who claims not to seek the truth, but already to possess it.—Romain Rolland

Thoughtful discussion requires direct teaching. Your advanced readers have mastered the mechanics of reading and, of course, the art of reading for pleasure. Your goal in adopting the Novel Approach is to lead them into a more intellectually rich form of reading. This analytical type of reading requires them to build new skills and, in particular, to test their thoughts and ideas in relation to those of others. This collaborative discussion is the key to the Novel Approach. Through it, your students go beyond their first impressions and singular thoughts. They begin to reason and to justify their thinking using evidence as much as logic. This is often new territory for advanced learners.

Entering into an intellectually rich discussion with others requires your students to be aware of what makes discussion effective. You probably have not thought of teaching students how to discuss, but the skills of discussion do not come naturally to young adolescents. Perceiving themselves as the center of the action, these youngsters are more likely to see a classroom discussion as either a questions/answer session with you as the leader and questioner or a time in which students are free to share their own thinking without listening too closely to what others have to say.

Don't expect your middle grade students to be comfortable with the Novel Approach type of discussion at first. Most of them are quite adept at expressing their views and presenting information they have conscientiously gathered. After all, they have had their share of "book reports" and other presentations of their own research efforts, complete with multimedia aids. Few of them have had the guidance and the opportunity to engage in a thoughtful discussion that encourages multiple points of view related to a reading. After all, the author has not presented a guidebook to analyzing his or her novel. The author has not directly shared the deeper meaning of the story nor the importance of pivotal events, characters, and "text" messages. What the reader gains from the reading of the novel can stay totally personal or it can become a vehicle for thinking aloud with others. That is the goal of the Novel Approach: reading for thinking.

A two-part lesson on developing effective reading discussion skills is included starting on page 60 of this section. You will find the lesson introduces your students to all of the essential components of an effective discussion. Your students need to internalize what makes a good discussion and what role they will play in ensuring its success.

Using the lesson for practice and modeling will make the transition to the Novel Approach discussions much stronger.

THE NOVEL APPROACH DISCUSSION CIRCLE

The center of success in using the Novel Approach is the discussion circle, a regularly scheduled gathering of the small group of students who are reading the same novel. This time for sharing ideas and images, guided by teacher-chosen discussion questions, enhances each student's perception of events and characters up to that point in the novel. The key elements of an effective discussion circle include the group members, the focus questions, the student preparation, the circle leadership, the interaction of the participants, and the individual and group reflections.

The Process

The discussion circle is student led and student assessed. The teacher observes the interaction and serves as a facilitator as needed. The students have received the focus questions prior to reading and they come to the circle ready to share their ideas related to each question. The student discussion leader begins by asking the first question. Students are encouraged to share their responses and their general thoughts and feelings about the novel, using a conversational tone. Besides their response to the question, students also indicate the page and paragraph where they found support for their response. Other students agree or disagree, also citing places in the text for their thoughts. When comments on the first question are exhausted, the leader moves the focus to the next question, and so on until the group has completed its discussion of the questions. Students learn to accept the opinions of others and practice the fine art of courteous disagreement as well as the skill of listening to others' comments to add more details or information without repetition. At all times members may request the citation (page, paragraph) from the book to clarify an answer or an interpretation.

The leader encourages all members to contribute, keeps the discussion moving, and guides the group assessment of the discussion period. At the conclusion of the allotted time for discussion, the leader asks the group members to reflect on their personal contributions and then suggests a summary rating for the group session. Forms for leader and individual student assessments of the discussion are included on pages 16–17.

Summary Guidelines for Novel Circle Discussions

How do students learn to participate in real novel discussion circles that are thoughtful and meaningful to all of the group members? A number of factors must be in place.

1. Whether the novel is assigned or chosen, the text must be engaging, complex, and contain powerful language. The students must be motivated enough by the content to read thoughtfully.

2. The discussion group should be small enough for full participation. About 4–8 students is the right number. You may have several small-group discussions occurring simultaneously.

3. The student preparations, based on open-ended questions, must be specific, purposeful, and useful for the discussion.

4. The leadership of the first discussion should be assigned to a student who is well prepared to lead. You may need to be the initial facilitator until students "get" the idea of shared, conversational discussion. In subsequent meetings, the leadership should rotate among group members.

5. Guidelines on "how to discuss" must be taught, practiced, and internalized.

6. Students must actively promote inclusive discussion and thoughtful connections to others' comments.

7. All members of the group must accept responsibility for the success of the discussion.

8. Focus questions must guide the discussion but not hamper it. Student comments and personal questions may direct discussion toward other topics and questions.

9. The discussion must include time for reflection and summarizing.

10. Time allotted for discussion should allow for ample responses from the group. Thoughtful, connected discussion cannot be rushed.

11. Individuals should reflect on their contributions and the leader should reflect on quality of the group's discussion.

12. The teacher must monitor and intervene as necessary to model effective discussion.

Student Guidelines for Novel Discussions

1. Get the right book.

2. Identify your discussion group.

3. Prepare for the group discussion.

4. Be a good leader or a great participant.

5. Practice good discussion skills.

6. Contribute your ideas.

7. Encourage others and connect with their thoughts.

8. Be prepared to ask a thoughtful question.

9. Think about ways you would summarize the group's discussion.

10. Reflect on your own contributions to the discussion. How can you improve?

Practice Lesson Part A

The Art and Practice of Effective Group Discussion

As students read and prepare for the discussion group they should be taught how to engage in a thoughtful small-group discussion. The following lesson is a good start.

Objective

Prepare students to participate in an effective novel discussion through learning the key elements of a successful group discussion and practicing their use.

Lesson at a Glance

+ Students discover key factors in a good discussion.
+ Students generate a list of important guidelines for an effective novel circle discussion.

Key Ideas to Develop

1. Different forms of classroom talk have different purposes.
2. Effective discussions require specific actions from each member of the group.
3. Thoughtful sharing of ideas in a group requires conversational style of speech.
4. In thoughtful discussions students build upon each other's ideas.

Instructions

1. Prepare a set of large cards with the following words:
    + Bored, distracted
    + Interrupter
    + Silent member
    + Off topic
    + Unprepared
    + Reciting to teacher

Prior to the lesson, select six students to simulate a poor discussion. Show each student one of the six cards and tell him or her to remember that this is the role he or she should play in the poor discussion. Let students know that everyone in the class will read a brief article, but only the group of six will have an opportunity to discuss it. Tell the six that when it is time for the discussion, they should act their roles out in an exaggerated way so the class can notice what they are doing as ineffective group members. Provide all students with a brief article to read (see 5 Elements That Make Fantasy Fiction Feel Real handout).

1. Tell students to read the article, highlighting interesting words and ideas. Allow time for the reading and highlighting.

2. Invite the six selected students to the front of the room where they will sit in a circle, not revealing their roles directly. Direct them to discuss the article as you ask key questions of them and they role-play the assigned interactions. Guide the discussion for about 10 minutes, allowing the six students to play out their assigned roles. Thank the participants and ask them to remain in their circle.

3. Tell the class that this discussion is not really about the article but about effective group discussions. Ask them to turn to a partner and consider how the group members helped or hindered the discussion. Allow a few minutes and then ask for contributions to a class chart, recording a summary of their comments, entitled, "What Makes an Unsuccessful Group Discussion."

4. After completing the chart, hold up each of the role cards and ask the class to identify which student was playing that ineffective role. Ask if any other comments should be added to the chart.

5. Tell students that they will be using discussion circles in their studies, specifically to discuss novels read for class. Ask them to help develop a class chart that has a new heading, "What Makes a Successful Group Discussion." Guide students to include the following ideas in their class-developed chart.
   + Everyone is prepared.
   + Everyone participates.
     - Everyone stays on topic.
     - Everyone explores issues in depth.
     - No one dominates the discussion.
     - No one interrupts.
     - You do not raise hands.
     - You speak to the group, not to the teacher.

   + You respond to each other's ideas.
   + You use verbal and nonverbal cues.

6. **Reflection.** Provide students with a copy of the Thoughtful Discussions Require handout. Let students know that this discussion practice will prepare them for discussions of actual content where the focus is on really analyzing what is written. In the future novel discussion, they will be asked to concentrate on preparing for a thoughtful discussion of what everyone has read. They will use their guidelines for successful discussion but will need to add some "thinking about the reading" elements.

   Briefly review each of the elements of a thoughtful discussion on the handout. This will enable students to begin thinking about their responsibilities for deeply analyzing the ideas in a reading and then sharing and connecting their thoughts.

7. Direct students to work with a partner to record a statement for each of the required elements of a thoughtful discussion, specifying what each of the elements would look like in a real discussion. When each student has completed

the sheet, ask student to personally rate each of the elements from 1–3 for how challenging that might be for them in a real discussion.

When students have finished the assignment, ask for volunteers to comment on the elements, giving examples of what it looks like in a real discussion. Summarize the discussion by asking volunteers to offer a reason why a student might rate one of the elements a 1 or a 3. This discussion will enable students to recognize that they are not alone if they are uncomfortable speaking out in groups, have a hard time finishing preparation assignments, or like to speak more than listen, for example.

5 Elements That Make Fantasy Fiction Feel Real

by Robert Liparulo

I like stories that surprise me, show me things I've never seen before, and get me playing make-believe like I haven't since selling my G.I. Joes and LEGOs at a garage sale.

Few tales are as make-believe (or as fun) as fantasy fiction—from the ones I call "light fantasy," like alternate histories, time travel, and monsters in the "real" world, to the hard-core stuff involving space odysseys, made-up worlds, and dragons.

Trouble is, I'm a skeptic, a hard sell. For a story to grab me, no matter how far-fetched it's supposed to be, I have to see and feel things I recognize, things I relate to.

Sounds like common sense, but as a voracious reader of published fiction and a judge in umpteen writing competitions, I'm here to tell you it's not as common as you'd think. If the first half of a book has left you thinking, I can't get my head around this, or more simply, Oh, come on!—then you know what I mean.

The idea of reality-based fantasy truly hit home when, after writing three thrillers for adults I decided to tackle a fantasy-adventure story for young adults.

In the Dreamhouse Kings series, a family moves to a small town in northern California, so Dad could take a job as principal of the local middle and high school. They move into a run-down Victorian home, where they find a hidden hallway of doors. Each door leads to a portal to a different time in history.

But not only can they go from the house to the past, people from the past can come through into their house. Someone does—and kidnaps Mom, taking her into some unknown place in the past. The family—primarily brothers David and Xander—begin a quest for Mom, which takes them to all sorts of dangerous and fascinating places throughout time. We slowly learn that the Kings are in the house for a very specific purpose, and they must do much more than "simply" find their mother.

My goal was to make the story feel as real as possible, to entice readers not only to enjoy my story of time travel, but to think maybe . . . just maybe, this could really happen. Well, I'd settle for their wishing it was real—and that they were part of the adventure. And just to set the target a bit higher, I wanted to reach even readers who don't normally like fantasy elements in stories; I wanted them to be surprised by how much they liked it.

In crafting the story, I identified a few key ingredients that would help me reach this goal. These aren't new ideas; many writers have used them to handhold readers into brilliant tales of fantasy. (And even non-fantasy authors incorporate them to varying degrees, but I believe fantasy writers need to be all the more aware of them and wield them more deliberately.) If you're a writer, consider making a mental checklist from these "tips of the trade."

CHAPTER 4 Materials

As a reader, you may benefit from knowing what's drawing you into a story . . . or why it's not working. So, here's what I look for:

1. **Characters who feel**. The way to a reader's heart is through a story's characters. Doesn't matter if they're fighting dragons or stepping into the Roman Colosseum during a gladiator fight, a character has to experience fear and courage, love and heartbreak, blood, sweat and tears—all of it realistically rendered in a way the reader understands. In the Dreamhouse Kings, I decided to make the time travel parts feel real by making everything else absolutely real.

2. **A character who's skeptical**. I believe some authors have done so much research and spent so much time contemplating the fantasies of their stories that buying into the fantastic is a no-brainer for them. Their characters barely shrug at the concept of vampires or the shattering of the laws of physics. I read a lot of fantasy, but I still want to be convinced every time. It helps when at least one character mirrors my disbelief. It tells me the author knows he or she is venturing into fantasy territory, so I trust that I won't be left behind. In other words, the author builds a bridge between reality and fantasy—if not necessarily with rock-solid explanations, then at least with feasible theories and suppositions.

3. **A learning curve in understanding the fantasy**. "Hey, a watch that stops time— let's do it!" You've probably seen the equivalent of this many times: the characters instantly grasp and use some crazy new item or idea. I want to see them stumble, misuse it, make mistakes, figure it out. In Richard Matheson's *I Am Legend* (my favorite book), protagonist Robert Neville is constantly learning new things about the creatures after him and the virus that turned them into vampire-like beasts. Readers get to tag along and figure out the problems and solutions with him; discovery becomes a team effort between character and reader.

4. **Real surroundings and situations**. Like characters who laugh and cry, hyperrealistic environments make the fantasy elements feel more real—because everything else is. When the King family finds the house, it's dusty and run down, the banister leaves splinters in their palms, when the electricity comes on, old bulbs pop.

5. **Consistency**. Readers of time-travel stories don't want to be told that technology can't be used in times before it was invented, and then read later how our hero uses a machinegun against Genghis Khan.

Not every story requires equal doses of these elements. Think of them as spices: the amount authors use of each depends on the dish they're preparing . . . and their personal tastes.

Note. "5 Elements That Make Fantasy Fiction Feel Real" by Robert Liparulo, 2010, retrieved from http://www.novelrocket.com/2010/06/5-elements-that-make-fantasy-fiction.html. Copyright 2010 by Robert Liparulo. Adapted with permission.

Practice Lesson Part B
The Art and Practice of Effective Group Discussion

Part B of the lesson provides students with practice in effective discussion.

Lesson at a Glance

+ Students review key factors in a good discussion.
+ Students prepare responses to two questions about the reading.
+ Students practice locating reading passages that support responses to higher level questions.
+ Students practice and assess the group discussion.

Key Ideas to Develop

1. Thoughtful sharing of ideas in a group requires careful preparation.
2. In thoughtful discussions, students build upon each other's ideas.
3. Students provide evidence for their ideas and opinions.
4. All members of a group are responsible for the discussion.
5. Leadership in a discussion circle may be assumed by any member and does not rest with the teacher.

Instructions

1. Ask students to retrieve the reading they completed in Part A of the discussion lesson. Post two open-ended questions and direct students to prepare responses to these questions by recording their ideas and the location of the evidence from the reading. They should list the page, the paragraph number, the first two words of the sentence, and a brief note to remind them of their thoughts. Allow time for this preparation.
2. Invite students to join small groups for the discussion. Appoint a leader for each group, reviewing the requirements for leaders and group participants posted on chart paper or provided on paper to students.
3. Let students know that they should follow the guidelines for a group discussion and be sure to help everyone contribute their ideas. Allow time for discussion
4. Following the discussion time, ask the students and the leader to complete assessments of their activity.
5. Reflect with the students on their successes and challenges, asking them which of the requirements was the most difficult to attain. Make suggestions for future successful group discussion. Keep charts with responsibilities for future use.

CHAPTER 4 Materials

6. Post this quotation and ask students to think about what it might mean. Briefly discuss this quote in terms of effective group discussion: "Discussion is an exchange of knowledge; argument is an exchange of ignorance"—Robert Quillen

Thoughtful Discussions Require

Element	Looks Like	Rating
Preparation		
Leadership		
Listening and Sharing		
Elaborating		
Summarizing		
Reflecting		

Chapter 5
Building Concepts and Vocabulary

> Every word or concept, clear as it may seem to be, has only a limited range of applicability.—Werner Heisenberg

What is the best way to improve the vocabulary of your advanced students? Even though they amaze you with their knowledge of words, that does not mean that they are "finished" with vocabulary development! Continuing instruction ensures that students not only discover new words and ideas but that their facility with multiple meanings and deep conceptualization grows. Research studies show that students learn more vocabulary informally or incidentally in the classroom than through traditional skill-building methods. Students increase their working vocabularies through frequent independent reading, listening to reading passages, and group discussion of what they have read.

The real key to effective vocabulary development is student use in context. The Novel Approach directs your students to recognize new words and phrases within the context of novel passages, read selected passages aloud, and then, in small groups, collaboratively internalize the meaning of the words as the author has used them. When students prepare for their regular novel discussion circle, part of the preparation is the building of a vocabulary list. As they come upon words during their reading that are new or interesting to them, they record those words. You should select a specific option for students to use in maintaining lists of their vocabulary words. Three options for students are suggested:

1. **Option 1:** Direct students to prepare a vocabulary section in their notebooks where they create a table for recording weekly vocabulary words. Words are added for each reading section. The table should look like this:

Page	Paragraph	Word	Meaning in Context

The notebook can be a composition book, spiral notebook, folder, or looseleaf binder.

2. **Option 2:** Provide students with a copy of an electronic file containing a table similar to the one in the first option or direct them to create their own file. Students add new words to the file each week.
3. **Option 3:** Require students to keep a personal word file box. Students record vocabulary words on 3" x 5" index cards, one per word. They include the word, the page and paragraph where it was found in the novel, and the definition as used in the context of the novel passage. Students file cards alphabetically.

Students should use reference tools for word meanings including dictionaries, both print and online. You may also require students to cite the word's origin, similar words, antonyms, or other information about each word. The important thing is to be sure they have come to an understanding of the word in the context it was used.

THE DISCUSSION CIRCLE VOCABULARY CHALLENGE

During the first few minutes of each novel group meeting, students take turns challenging members of the group to explain the meaning of the selected word or term as it is used in the book. The group must agree to the explanation. This process promotes deep understanding of the vocabulary the author has chosen to use in the novel. By first coming to a personal understanding of the word, the student has a fairly good understanding of the passage in which the word was used. By challenging others to explain and elaborate on their understanding, the student is deepening his own understanding while also enabling the group to come to a consensus definition. The purposeful use of words in context is a powerful way of strengthening learning and in the process students enjoy trying to stump each other on choice words. Words unfamiliar to the group are bound to come up through this activity.

By selecting their own word and phrases, students are much more likely to "own" the word and find motivation to really understand what it means. They begin to see the importance of precision in word selection and come to understand that the novelist seeks words that convey very precise meanings, enabling the reader to experience rich imagery from the printed page. As their teacher, you can convey an interest and delight in words and encourage students to make use of the words and phrases they meet throughout the day. Highlighting several by putting them on display provides both your students and you with a focus on purposeful yet informal use in context, the most effective way to increase vocabulary. You can provide a copy of the following note to students about the vocabulary list or use similar words to share the idea of the vocabulary challenge with them.

A Note to the Student: *Your Novel Vocabulary List*

You will be asked to collect vocabulary words and use them in different ways. The purpose of these activities is to help you become more aware of words and more adept at selecting particular words for particular purposes. The words you choose for your vocabulary list each week do not have to be the most difficult to pronounce or the longest words you can find. The best words to choose are those you have seen before but don't ordinarily use in your own speaking and writing. These words are ones you will probably meet again and it will be to your advantage to learn about them and their variations.

Sometimes you won't find any new words for your vocabulary list. In this case, just select the most interesting ones you can find. As you use them in the vocabulary activities, you are sure to find out something new.

A dictionary should be your friendly companion as you prepare your vocabulary work. You should also use a thesaurus to expand your understanding of the words you select. An interesting side effect of dictionary and thesaurus work is the extra information you will pick up along the way such as word origins, alternative uses, prefixes, and suffixes. Most of us cannot resist a peek at some other word or illustration that catches our eye. That's incidental learning. Enjoy!

VOCABULARY ACTIVITIES

Additional activities to deepen understanding of the words are provided in this chapter. These vocabulary and concept-building activities can be used with any section of the reading or, in fact, in any learning content area and context. The activities include a number of strategies that students should use over and over as support for individual growth in language. Assign these additional vocabulary-building activities as appropriate for your class. The strategies and activities include support for:

+ understanding in context,
+ analysis of word origins and structure,
+ relationships to other words,
+ concept development, and
+ precision in use.

Choosing learning activities that support vocabulary growth and conceptual development is like putting money in the bank. Growth with interest occurs when students manipulate their understanding of the words they meet so that they have a more precise command of these concepts now and in the future.

Analysis of Origins and Structure

Word etymology. Encourage your students to use the Internet to explore root words, meanings, origins, and suffixes to analyze word structure and word variations. The following websites are suggested:

1. *Learn That Word*: https://www.learnthat.org/pages/view/roots.html. This website is sponsored by a nonprofit foundation established to promote vocabulary development based on cognitive neuroscience and technology. Students can develop a personal word list and then use multisensory options on the website to practice word meanings. This site also includes extensive lists of root words, prefixes, and suffixes.

2. *Building Vocabulary: Prefixes, Roots, and Suffixes*: http://www.readingfirst. virginia.edu/elibrary_pdfs/Building_Vocabulary.pdf. At this website, students will find tables of prefixes, suffixes, and roots with their meanings and example words. You may download these pages and make multiple copies for educational purposes.

3. *Reading Rockets*: http://www.readingrockets.org/article/root-words-roots-and-affixes. Reading Rockets is a national multimedia literacy initiative. Its website offers reproducible lists of common Latin and Greek roots with definitions as well as common affixes, definitions, and examples.

Relationship to Other Words

Word cubes (played with partners). Provide each student group with a word cube on the faces of which you have written these words: analyze, define, apply, compare, relate, connect. Students take turns choosing one of their vocabulary words to share.

Rules:
1. First person selects a vocabulary word and tosses the cube.
2. Partner responds to the toss.
3. Score one point if response is correct. If incorrect, the student who shared the word gives a correct response and scores one point.
4. Play then goes to the partner to offer a word.
5. Play continues for six rounds. Note that not all faces may appear during the game. Also, the rules may be adjusted to allow for four or six players in the game.

The words on the cube relate to the following activities:
+ **Analyze:** What do you know about this word? Part of speech, origin, prefix/suffix, root.
+ **Define:** Give a definition for the word.
+ **Apply:** Use the word in an appropriate way in an original sentence.
+ **Compare:** Compare this word to some other word and explain why your comparison works.
+ **Relate:** Relate this word to some person, place, or event in the novel.
+ **Connect:** Connect this word to something in your own life.

Word webs (individual or partner). Students are asked to "web" their vocabulary word. The web is like a brainstorming on paper or free-flowing mapping of the word. Students start with a vocabulary word in a bubble in the center of the paper. They then create branches with connecting bubbles that could include antonyms, synonyms, illustrations, other forms of the word, definition, prefixes, suffixes, sentences, and figurative use. Students are challenged to make their webs as extensive as possible. Working with a partner stimulates broader thinking.

As an alternative web, the student may be directed to develop a web of specifics such as different meanings for this word with connected use in sentences or only different forms of the word.

Word links (individual and partner). Using a list of 10 words from this week's reading section, students form word links using random thoughts and ideas to connect one word to another in a chain. Students show their word chain on paper, then share their linking with a partner. Connections can be totally unusual as long as students can explain their reasons for making the connections.

CONCEPT DEVELOPMENT

One way to directly guide students to think about the meaning of certain concepts is to use the concept development method. This is especially helpful in supporting students' conception of big ideas, particularly as used in novel themes. Abstract ideas like liberty, power, and conflict can be explored for deep meaning and generalizations.

One way of guiding students to conceptual development is an adaptation of the work of Hilda Taba. This strategy engages students in inductive reasoning. Students make generalizations only after data are gathered and organized. The data gathering enables students to note the common characteristics of a concept.

Steps in the Concept Development Process

1. *Generate examples of the concept.* What are some examples of the concept? List them. Try for many examples.
2. *Group similar examples and develop categories.* Put like things together. Put every one of your examples into a category. Label the categories.
3. *Develop nonexamples.* Can you think of something similar that is just different enough that it is a nonexample?
4. *Create generalizations.* Now generate some statements about the concept that are just about always true in every situation.

The following example of a concept development learning activity with the word *conflict* illustrates this strategy.

The Conceptualization of Conflict

1. Provide each group with a large piece of chart paper and a marker and ask them to list as many examples of conflict as they can think of. Let them know that examples can come from their personal life, their community, the world, nature . . . any examples of conflict are acceptable.
2. Allow time for each group to record at least 15 examples of conflict. Then, ask students to look at their examples and think of different categories they can use to sort the examples. Ask them to designate different groups of conflicts and label them. They may use color-coding, letter designations, or some other method of grouping. Let them know that every example should be in a group. When students have their categories complete, ask groups to share their categories and note the similarities and differences among group reports. This step is crucial for concept development! Be sure students have the time to consider possible generalizations and then refine them to create

the class list. *Do not* provide them with a list, but guide their thinking as necessary.

3. Next, ask students to make a list of nonexamples of conflict. Acknowledge that this will be more difficult. After some thinking time, ask groups to share nonexamples. Say: *Can you think of a nonexample of conflict? Something that is similar in terms of a relationship or event but that is not exactly a conflict?* This is quite a challenge!

4. If students are having difficulty thinking of nonexamples, use the following examples to generate discussion.
   + Two students are having a discussion about which school has the best football team. (Just an opinion.)
   + Should I have chocolate ice cream or watermelon for dessert? (Just a choice.)
   + Not everyone likes the new school mascot. (Just an opinion.)

5. Once students have a set of categories (different types of conflict) as well as a few nonexamples of conflict, ask them to think of general statements that can be made about conflict. These are called *generalizations*, things that are just about always true about conflict. If necessary, provide an example: Conflicts can be brief or long lasting.

6. When groups have completed the task, record their ideas on chart paper and discuss. Establish a class set of generalizations about conflict that will likely include the following ideas: (1) conflicts arise from opposing ideas, resources, power, or status; (2) conflicts can be internal or external; (3) conflict resolution may be sought in violent or nonviolent ways; (4) conflicts may be resolved simply or may escalate over time; and (5) people often take sides in a conflict. Do not provide the list of generalizations, but rather work with the class to develop a set of general statements about conflict everyone agrees upon.

This strategy for concept development is particularly worthy of the time invested as you guide students to deeply understand some of the universal ideas that are key to novel themes. The following are some of those possible thematic concepts:

+ beauty	+ fortune	+ power
+ change	+ freedom	+ progress
+ darkness	+ heroism	+ self-reliance
+ duty	+ individualism	+ survival
+ deception	+ isolation	+ war
+ family	+ injustice	+ wisdom

Note that these concepts are universal. When you help your students to analyze them through the concept development model, the generalizations they form will be useful in expanding their ideas about the theme of each novel. Many other thematic topics are frequently used by authors, but this list is a good start. Remember that these are topics/concepts, not themes, although they are the underlying ideas within themes. A theme is the main idea an author conveys such as "Good triumphs over evil." The theme of a novel is the underlying layer of meaning in the whole novel.

Graphic Organizer for Concept Development

A variation on the concept development lesson is the use of graphic organizers that guide students through similar steps in conceptualization. A revision of the popular Frayer model for vocabulary development is shown in Figure 5. Note that students do not begin with the definition, but rather form a definition after having thought through the characteristics, examples, and nonexamples of the word. This encourages much thought about the idea before formulating a conclusion about meaning. The process should be done in a small group rather than as an independent activity so that students think aloud and benefit from expanding their own thinking through listening to and considering the ideas of others.

Ask students to complete a graphic organizer like the one in Figure 5 for selected vocabulary words. It is important that thinking go beyond the individual, so that each student's conceptual understanding is modified or reinforced. Completing the organizer alone does not allow for this active thinking. Direct students to first think of examples of the word and record them in the upper left quadrant. Next, students record what they know to be the characteristics of the chosen concept. These are recorded in the upper right quadrant. Thinking of nonexamples is difficult for students but it helps them to understand the difference between this concept and others closely related. For example, for the term *citizen*, a nonexample might be someone living in a country as a visitor. Finally, students form a definition of the concept that they can agree upon. Precision of language is developed here and students come away with a much clearer understanding of the concept.

PRECISION IN USE

Author's Choice (Individual, Group)

As an alternative to one of the open-ended questions provided in preparation for a novel discussion circle, direct students to look at the language the author used.

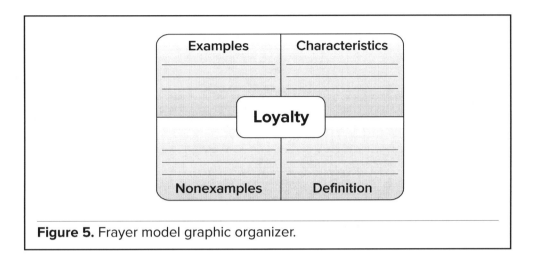

Figure 5. Frayer model graphic organizer.

Ask them to locate particular words, phrases, or sentences that highlight ways in which the author was quite precise in his or her selection of language to use. You may select from the following or develop you own student search for precise language.

1. Examine this section of the novel, looking for ways the author has used language to describe the characters.
2. Look for examples in words and phrases where the author established or changed the setting of the story.
3. Find examples in words and phrases that were used by the author to convey a particular mood.
4. Find examples of words and phrases that enabled you to know the feelings of a particular character. Indicate whether the author described the emotions or used dialogue to convey the emotions.
5. Find words and phrases that helped you to "see" a particular person, place, or thing in your mind. Look for vivid imaging.
6. Find examples of alliteration in this section.
7. Find words and phrases that the author uses to foreshadow the future in the story.

Linear Arrays

The development of a linear array is a strategy to extend precision in word choice by asking students to expand their understanding of subtle differences in words. Using opposites on each end, students add words that are in between those two in meanings (see Figure 6). The use of a thesaurus is quite helpful for this activity. Linear arrays are visual representations of degree. An activity like this helps students examine subtle distinctions in the words. Linear arrays may be more

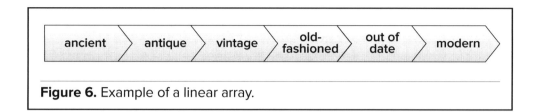

Figure 6. Example of a linear array.

appropriate for displaying other types of relationships among words. For example, many sets of words differ essentially in degree: annoyed, angry, enraged, and furious; or lukewarm, warm, hot, and scalding. The relationship among such words can be illustrated visually by arranging them in a line. Shades of meaning between the words are arranged according to degree of size, frequency, intensity, position, or chronology.

Try using the following words in linear arrays to show subtle changes in the meaning of words.

+ beautiful—ugly
+ never—always
+ delighted—displeased
+ blush—scarlet
+ include—exclude
+ lazy—energetic

Name: _____ Date: _____

Imaginative Comparisons

Similes and metaphors are used by authors to help the reader form more vivid mind pictures. Locate several examples from your reading. Remember that similes express comparisons using like or "as," while metaphors do not.

Page	Paragraph	Comparison	Simile or Metaphor?

Select a comparison from those you listed that is especially vivid in your mind. Illustrate the comparison on a separate sheet of paper or write in words the picture you see in your mind.

Alluring Alliteration

Saying the same sound at the start of several words in a series is an artful accent that adventuresome authors address as alliteration. This special play on sounds in words is a terrific technique for quietly highlighting particular passages in a radiant rhythm. Identify several alliterative passages from your reading and record them below.

Page	Paragraph	Alliteration

Now create some original alliterative phrases or sentences that relate to your reading. They may relate to one of the characters, an event, or the setting of the novel.

_____

_____

_____

_____

_____

Chapter **6**

The Elements of a Novel

> Basically, all novelists should want to tell a story, and if they don't want to, they shouldn't be novelists. I think story-telling is important and underrated.—Susan Howatch

When you read a novel, you often find some element particularly compelling. It may be an intriguing character or a unique period of time that grabs you. Perhaps it is the overall message of the story or the way the author uses language. Effective novelists leave little to chance but rather plan for all the elements of a novel as they weave a story worthy of a place on the library shelves, on your Kindle, and in people's hearts. An author sets out to tell a story and in the telling ensures that it all hangs together. A really good novel allows the reader to enter the author's world, make personal connections to the story, and leave the end of the book wanting more.

Your students will be better able to understand the meaning and the message of the author's words when they have familiarity with the structure of the novel. Although different novel genres focus on one or two elements more than others, all novels have a set of elements in common.

THE SETTING

Where and when the novel takes place, the setting, is the canvas upon which the author depicts the story. The setting allows the characters to come to life in an environment that is known to them and revealed to the reader. Sometimes the setting becomes the focus, central to the unfolding of the story, a time and place discovered or uncovered by the novel's characters. For example, a novel may take its characters into an uncharted world in which their actions and behaviors are dependent upon this new place. A setting may include a geographical location described in great detail or the setting may focus more on the daily living of the characters, their homes, and community landmarks. The setting may present the period of time in which the novel's action occurs. It may also incorporate the psychological environment of the characters including their moral, social, and emotional climate.

THE PLOT

The novelist has a story to tell. The plot is the key sequence of events that moves the story from beginning to end. Just like the foundation is the key to a strong house, the author's plot is the foundation of a novel. Strategic events that occur throughout the novel are the steps in the journey. Sometimes the situation changes, sometimes the characters change, and sometimes the writer reveals things along the way that change the reader's understanding of what is happening. The plot is always the unfolding of the story from start to finish. Central to the plot in most stories is the idea of conflict. This is the main dramatic factor within the story that is resolved in stages. The beginning of the story introduces the characters and establishes the tone for the story. This part of the plot is called the exposition. Continuing the story, rising action moves the plot along until the climax, which is the most significant, heightened, intense part of the novel. It is followed by falling action, the place in the plot where major changes occur, often in the main characters. The resolution of the plot is the next stage, generally resolving the conflict, issue, or mystery presented in the overall storyline (see Figure 7 for a diagram of plot). Novels typically end on a happy note, an unhappy conclusion, or an open-ended, ambiguous note.

THE CHARACTERS

It's all about the characters. Without them, a novel does not exist. With them, the reader begins to enter into the story through the character's thoughts, goals, and activities. A character may be immediately likeable or despicable. Connecting with the characters on an emotional level is the beginning of a reader's meaningful interaction with the story.

Generally there is a lead character, the protagonist. It is this central character upon whom the plot evolves. Sometimes we hear the voice of the protagonist as the teller of the story. Other characters presented in the novel round out the storyline and provide greater or lesser supporting roles for the main character(s). The antagonist is the one who causes the trouble in a novel. It may be a person, but could also

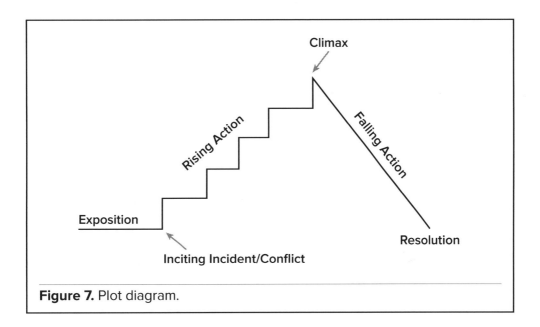

Figure 7. Plot diagram.

be a sense of evil, an illness, or some enormous challenge that blocks the progress of the main character's quest to achieve a goal. The antagonist does everything possible to inflict harm or cause conflict, seemingly relentless in this attempt. Other characters in the novel may be described as "round," those who are fairly well developed and serve key roles in the novel. These characters are part of the action and important to the storyline. A few other characters are described as "flat," those who have little dimension and no real role other than to keep the story going. They are the necessary people who typically would be part of the environment, like the bus driver or the school principal. They are like part of the scenery. Table 2 presents a listing and description of each type of character.

An outstanding novel includes characters who are more than believable. They are authentic. They are sincere. They are relatable. You would recognize them if you met them on the street. You can easily picture each character as part of the setting. Getting to know the characters is easy in a powerful novel. Although a character may evolve, the evolution is natural and connected to the unfolding story.

THE DIALOGUE

The conversation between characters in the novel is called the dialogue. Dialogue represents the actual words of the character. For example, one of the characters might say: "I think this is the right time to tell you about my uncle's secret past."

Table 2

Character Types

Character	Description
Protagonist	+ Lead character + Central to the story + Always involved in the conflict + Usually changes from beginning to end of story
Antagonist	+ Enemy of the protagonist + Blocks progress of lead character + May be a human, a force, or a circumstance
Round characters	+ Round out the story + Key players in the plot + Are active and well defined
Flat characters	+ Necessary to the setting + One- or two-dimensional + Not central to the action

Dialogue cues guide you to recognize who is speaking. Such cues are "he said," "she replied," or longer phrases like, "Thomas let Jim know his feelings when he said, 'I believe in you.'"

Dialogue makes a novel come alive. It allows you as the reader to learn more about the characters' personalities and ways of thinking as you "hear" their words. It is like listening in to people's conversations without actually being a part of the action.

When a novel is effective, the dialogue seems natural to the characters and to the story. It is important, bringing drama to the events that carry the story along. The story's dialogue may reveal more about the personality and thinking of the characters. It may also serve to convey the action in the story.

THE POINT OF VIEW

An author makes a choice about how the story will be told, the narration. The choice enables the author to purposefully decide what the reader should know throughout the story. The author also uses it to reveal the characters' feelings about the situations that unfold. Point of view generally involves the selection of narration from one of three different perspectives, described in Table 3. You may wonder about use of second person in narratives. If you were to scan thousands of novels, looking for the point of view used by the authors, you would likely not find the use of second person ("you") in even one. This is because the use of second person

Table 3

Points of View

Point of View	Description
First person narrative	+ One person is the storyteller sharing personal point of view + May be the central character or another character + Narrator says, "I" + Reader only knows this person's side of the story
Third person limited narrative	+ Storyteller is not a character in the story + Storyteller tells things known by one character + Storyteller only knows about one character's inner thoughts and feelings + Storyteller says "He" or "She"
Third person all-knowing (omniscient) narrative	+ Storyteller is not a part of the story + Storyteller is omniscient (i.e., knows all) + Storyteller can share information about everyone and everything + Storyteller may describe events, thoughts, and feelings as well as dialogue

requires the reader to suspend reality and pretend to be the "you" in the novel. As an example, a second person narrative might begin, "You are the type of person who enjoys teasing others." This perspective would be different for every reader and so novelists stick to use of first or third person, allowing the reader to witness the events of the story rather than attempt to be a direct part of it.

THE THEME

Upon reading a novel, you often notice a pattern of thought which brings you, as the reader, to analyzing broader life issues. This is the underlying theme or message that conveys an opinion about human nature or societal values. Not to be confused with the plot, the storyline that unfolds, the theme is what the reader takes away as a lasting lesson from the story. It represents the author's overall message in writing this novel. Remind students that:

+ The plot conveys the actions of the characters.
+ The theme conveys the underlying message.

Here are some examples of themes that may be used in novels:

+ To have a friend, you must be a friend.
+ Friends and acquaintances come and go, but family connections are everlasting.

+ The patterns found in nature are often reflected in human behaviors.
+ Human beings have universal needs that must be priorities in their lives.
+ Crime does not pay.
+ Conflict is often present between man and nature.
+ Hard work turns adversity into triumph.
+ People are shaped by the circumstances around them.
+ People can change their lives for the better.

Some common topics related to themes include:
+ family and love;
+ life, birth, death;
+ power;
+ heroism;
+ war and peace;
+ hope and hopelessness;
+ journey;
+ coming of age;
+ fortune;
+ isolation;
+ hope and triumph;
+ self-discoveries; and
+ cultural influences.

Note that a topic is not a theme, but every theme is related to a universal, over-arching topic. Themes are open to interpretation, so readers can find different ways of looking at the overall deeper meaning, message, or theme of the book. The plot entertains, but the theme helps the reader develop a deeper understanding of some part of everyday life

The following learning activities may be used in conjunction with a study of the elements of a novel.

Probing Questions

A good researcher is first of all a probing questioner. Practice in forming interesting questions is time well spent. If the author of your novel were available, what questions would you want to ask? Prepare a set of questions that others who read this author's works would find interesting.

_____

_____

_____

_____

_____

Is it possible to get your questions answered? Do some research on the author to determine the answer. If so, how will you go about it?

_____

_____

_____

_____

_____

_____

_____

Reading Section Pyramid

Build a pyramid summary of the section of the book you were assigned. In the outline, place one word for a central character, two words to show feelings the character revealed, three words to describe where the main action took place, four words to tell an important event, and five words to tell about a conflict or problem that still exists.

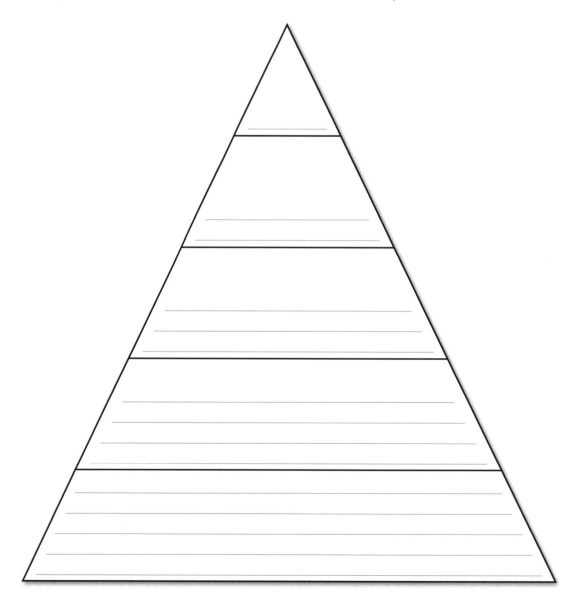

Name: _____ Date: _____

Episode Analysis

Choose some part of your reading where the main character was confronted with some decision or experienced some event. On the graphic below, record the episode in brief sentences, describing the event and the results of the event for the main character.

Initiating Event: What was the circumstance that caused this event to happen?
Reaction of Main Character: How did the main character react? Did the character do something?
Action of Main Character: What did the main character do as a result of what happened?
Consequences: What was the outcome?

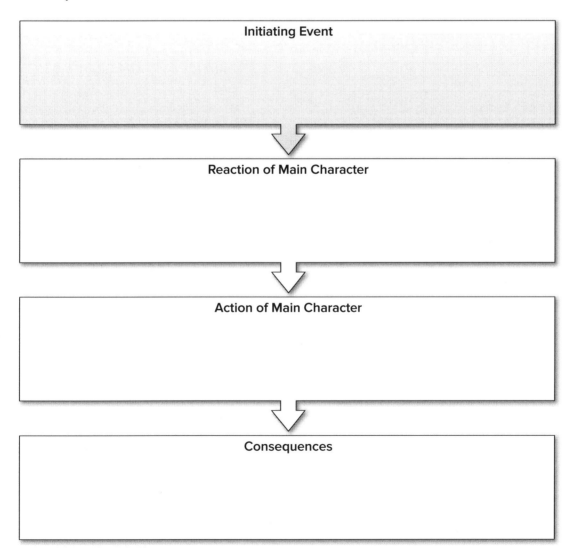

Initiating Event

Reaction of Main Character

Action of Main Character

Consequences

Character Profile

Choose a protagonist and create a main character profile. Continue to add to this profile as you read through the novel. You may draw a picture of the character and add various dimensions of the character's personality as they are revealed. Be as descriptive as possible in your choice of words. Include things such as physical appearance, habits, personality traits, hobbies, interests, and typical expressions the character uses.

Character Comparison

Choose two round characters from your novel. They may be closely related, friends, or enemies. Use the Venn diagram to describe similarities and differences between the two characters. Consider things like appearance, personality, experiences, and interests. Do you remember what makes a character a round character? Record your definition.

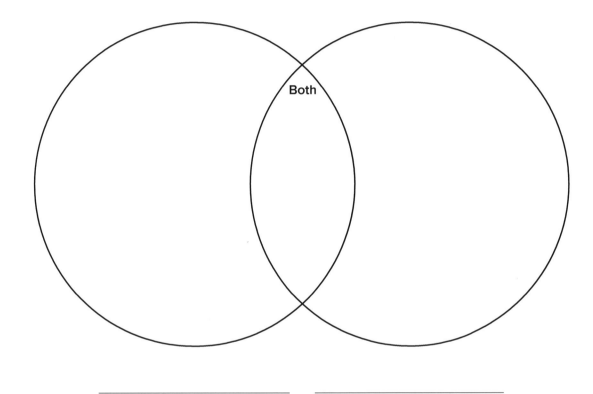

Both

_____   _____

Name: _____ Date: _____

Character Quotes

Select several characters from your book. From the reading you have already done, choose a quote from each person that seems to say something important, either directly or indirectly. Then locate a famous quotation or saying that you feel each character would choose as important.

Character:	
Character's Quote:	**Famous Quote or Saying:**

Character:	
Character's Quote:	**Famous Quote or Saying:**

Character:	
Character's Quote:	**Famous Quote or Saying:**

Character Tree

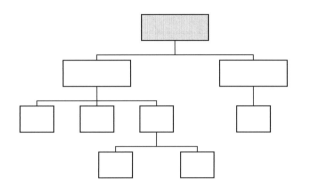

Design a character tree similar to a family tree, but showing the various branches as important people in a central character's life. Perhaps one branch would show family (or would this be your character's root system?), and another branch might show work or school friends.

Be very creative and imaginative as you create your tree. Consider showing special features such as blossoms, fruit, blight, fallen leaves, various seasons, weather, or the time of day to symbolize the variety of relationships.

Other Character Projects

Character Collage: Create a collage of words and pictures to convey the personality of your favorite character. Use a computer or create it on paper.

T-Shirt: A T-shirt can convey a special message or a personal idea. Design a T-shirt picture and slogan that is just right for one of your novel's characters. You may choose to actually complete this on a real T-shirt or on paper.

What's in _____'s Bag?: Select a character and create a bagful of possessions for that person. Present it in any way you choose: words, pictures, dramatic display of real items, a computer-generated graphic, and so on.

Their Favorite Things: Choose two characters. Make lists of their favorite things, places, sayings, and friends. Note any items they seem to have in common. What do these lists tell about the personalities of each character? Write briefly about each person, describing each in general.

Character Time Capsule: Think about things that are very important to one or more of the characters. Consider items that would be of lasting significance to them. Select five things you think the character would have placed in a time capsule to be left for future people to open 100 years from the time of placement. Write a couplet (two-line rhyming poem) to accompany each item.

Character Yes or No: This is a game of "guess the character," which can be played in a small or large group. Names of characters are placed into a container. One student draws a character's name and responds with only "yes" or "no" answers to questions from the group members. The first person to guess the correct character may draw the next name.

Variation: Questioners may ask only questions that deal with the character's feelings.

Character Silhouette: Choose a character. List adjectives that most closely fit that person. Write a physical description of the character you have selected. Try to limit your writing to exactly 35 words.

Character Simile: Make a list of words useful in describing a person's appearance. Then make a list of words useful in describing a person's feelings. Now create similes about a character, choosing a word from the appearance list or one from the feelings list as starters. For example, you might write, "Harry was as angry as a full-blown tornado" or "Mila was as tall as a skyscraper."

Add a Character: Think about a famous person you feel could be smoothly written into your novel in a "cameo" appearance. Be sure the person is of the correct time period or is appropriate for the setting of the novel. Find out enough about the famous person to decide how, when, and where you could write him or her into the action. Write about it or write a scene for the person to dramatize.

Peas in a Pod and Polar Opposites: Pair up your favorite novel character with real-life people who would be good personality match-ups—Peas in a Pod! Next, choose some real-life people who would be at the opposite end of the "pole" in personality from a favorite character—Polar Opposites!

Role Listing: People are very complex and engage in various roles during the same time frame. For example, you may be a student, a soccer player, a friend, a pet owner, a group leader, a dishwasher, an artist, etc. Choose a character from your reading and make role lists, one for you and one for the character. When the lists are complete, compare them. Check any roles you have in common. Circle those that are favorites. Star the least favorites. Put a D beside the most difficult roles.

Cinquain a Character: A cinquain poem has five lines. It has a definite pattern, but does not require rhyme. Select a book character. Try to capture something special about that character in a cinquain. Then write a cinquain about yourself, using the example below.

Line one: one word   Michael
Line two: two words   Gentle giant
Line three: three words   Helping many people
Line four: four words   His courage is mighty
Line five: one word   Policeman

Name: _____ Date: _____

Name It

Authors face a very important decision when selecting a book title. Readers are frequently turned on to a book simply by knowing its title. Think about the novel you are reading and make a list of other possible titles. Star the one that appeals to you the most. Take an informal survey of others who have read this book and place a check mark beside their favorites from your list.

_____

_____

_____

_____

_____

Can you think of an important consideration in selecting a particular book title? This is a criterion or standard any title would have to possess. Think of at least one criterion for a title.

_____

_____

_____

_____

_____

What's in a Chapter?

Authors have definite reasons for separating their works into chapters. Look over the last two chapters from your novel and consider the reasoning behind the chapter division. Tell why you think it makes sense to end at that particular point. If you disagree with the division tell why.

_____

_____

_____

_____

_____

_____

_____

_____

_____

Special Places

What are the special places mentioned in this section of the novel? Can you visualize them? Choose one of the following activities:

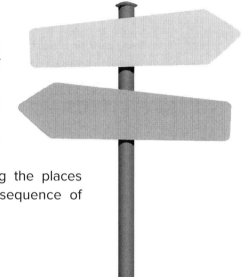

1. Design a map with symbols for each important location.
2. Create a sketch or drawing showing one place. Elaborate and show many details.
3. Show a footstep progression picture naming the places a main character visited. Use the correct sequence of movements.

Interesting Interviews

To get a profile of one of your novel's characters, work with a partner to improve your interviewing techniques. One of you will assume the character's role, and the other will conduct the interview.

The person representing the character should review book passages to prepare for questions on the thoughts, personality, and problems of the character. The person who will conduct the interview should plan ahead to decide on important areas for discussion. Four or five probing questions should work as a guide for discussion.

During the interview, a character may elaborate on an area and give more details than the book offers, but should stay within reasonable bounds for what the character would probably say. A true attempt should be made at really visualizing and assuming the role.

The interviewer should complete note taking in any form that is comfortable. Following the interview, the information gathered should be organized and prepared for presentation. Write up the interview and combine it with others done in the class to complete a magazine similar to *People*. Examine an issue to determine what words and graphics to include. Students not responsible for recording interviews should assume other roles and responsibilities for the production of the magazine. List tasks to be completed and assign jobs. Be sure to select a deadline. Post the final magazine on a class webpage or blog.

Philosophy of Life

Often the reading of a book helps us to sort out our feelings about things. When we have a set of beliefs and values that seem to stay the same, we are beginning to develop a personal philosophy.

Meet with your group to discuss what it means to have a philosophy of life. Seek help from your teacher or other sources such as books or Internet searches if you seem to need help getting started. When you have a good understanding of this idea, choose a book character who seems to have a philosophy similar to your own or who seems to have influenced your personal feelings and beliefs, either positively or negatively.

On a separate piece of paper, record the things you think that character values or believes. Combine your ideas into a well-formed paragraph that indicates the character's philosophy of life. Now form another paragraph that reflects your personal philosophy of life.

Clues to Time

How does the author handle the passage of time in your novel? Find time words or references in the current section you are reading and write them below.

_____

_____

_____

_____

_____

Decide on a visual way to show the passage of time in this section of your novel or in the entire book up to this point. Perhaps you would like to create a timeline or show the time passing on a clock face. Maybe you have some other way to show it. Be creative!

Problem Solving

Understanding how characters solve problems can help you to analyze real-life situations. Choose a dilemma or problem presented in your novel. Think about the details of the problem like what caused it, who was involved, and how it was handled. Record the details below.

The problem:

_____

Facts:

_____

_____

_____

If the problem was resolved or something happened to lessen it, what happened?

_____

_____

_____

What other ideas would you have for solving the same problem?

_____

_____

_____

What do you think is the most practical solution to a problem like this?

_____

_____

_____

Where Am I?

Think about the places described in your novel. Invent a humorous character who will visit these places. Prepare a written description to present to your group. The first part should introduce the new character in detail and the rest of the writing should lead you all on an adventure to familiar places from the novel with your new character.

_____

_____

_____

_____

_____

_____

_____

_____

_____

Other Places, Other Times

Select items from this reading section that would not exist or would definitely be different if the story were set in a different place or time. Think up another place or time and a replacement item for each. For example, if you were reading about a character's use of her computer, how would that be different in a historical novel set in 1805?

Item From Novel	Other Place or Time	Replacement Item

Hot and Cold

If asked our feelings about a particular book, we often haven't stopped long enough to analyze our general reactions. This exercise is designed to help you sort out your emotional responses to one section of your novel.

1. For each page of your reading, mark a number 1 to 10, weak to strong, to show your level of feelings when you read that page.
2. Add up all the ratings and find your average feelings rating.
3. Select two pages to which you gave a high or a low rating and tell what prompted your emotional response.

A Novel Museum

Future generations would like to remember the happenings from this novel by visiting a museum of artifacts.

Each member of your group should select 3–5 important items to display. In addition, each member should record 3–5 important facts.

The entire group should decide where and how the museum display is to be set up. Tour guides should prepare a brief talk to accompany the display.

Date for display: _____

Items to be displayed:_____

_____

_____

_____

_____

Interesting facts: _____

_____

_____

_____

_____

If a real display is not possible, sketch or create scale drawings of the display.

Name: _____ Date: _____

Be a Friend

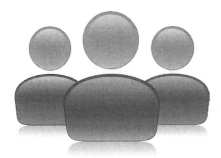

When we are faced with a problem, it often helps to get some good advice from a friend. What sort of problems has one of your book characters faced lately? Write a letter to him or her, giving encouragement or advice as you would to a good friend.

_____

_____

_____

_____

_____

_____

_____

_____

_____

Speed Skimming

Work with your group taking turns reading short parts from this week's reading. After a section is read aloud, other group members race to skim material and locate the page and paragraph. Give five points to the person who locates the passage first, four points for the second person, and three points for the third. Continue to play until everyone has had a chance to read a section. Total up points to determine the skimming champ.

Listing Ideas for Fluent, Flexible Thinkers

1. List every character.

2. List ways your novel says "said."

3. List any foods mentioned in the book.

4. List ways the author shows size.

5. Write a problem solved in your novel. List other ways it could have been solved.

6. Open your novel to any page. Find the name of an object. Make that your list heading. List uncommon uses for the item.

7. List happy thoughts about your novel.

8. List places mentioned in the novel.

9. List ideas or things you think the author of this novel believes.

10. List the best places to read a novel like this.

More Creative Explorations

1. Select a passage that makes you feel a particular emotion. Locate a work of music that gives you a similar feeling. Reread the passage as you listen to the music in the background. Do you find that the feeling you have grows more intense? Would the music you selected provide a good background for a dramatization of the passage? Test your opinion on a friend to see if you both reach the same conclusions.

2. Make a series of abstract drawings in color to accompany several passages that give you strong feelings. Show your drawings to a friend to see if your particular feelings "show" in the pictures.

3. Work with a partner or small group. Take turns reading aloud short passages that make the reader feel something. Those listening should express their feelings through facial expressions and body movements (placement, posture, dance, or a combination).

4. If your favorite character wrote a book, what would it be about? What would the title be?

5. Draw a sketch about the most humorous or interesting part of your reading.

6. Make a commercial for selling your book.

7. Make a felt board picture story to tell the novel in simplified form.

8. Create new names for the characters that reflect their personalities (for example, Ima Bird, B. A. Baker, Justin Time).

9. Create an original book jacket.

10. Make new lyrics to a familiar tune like "Row, Row, Row, Your Boat" to tell about your story in song.

11. Write an incident into a dramatic scene. Act it out.

12. Create a photo journal of some special story incidents.

13. Dramatize your vocabulary words.

14. Write a limerick about a favorite character.

15. Sketch a building described in the story.

16. In a group, pantomime a story scene for others to identify.

17. Create a puppet show.

18. Think of other uses for your book besides reading it that would not destroy the book.

Chapter 7

The Realistic Novel

> It's no wonder that truth is stranger than fiction. Fiction has to make sense.—Mark Twain

Believable situations . . . ordinary people . . . current times . . . realistic novels are about everyday life. The characters are fictionalized, yet appear to be people you might know, dealing with issues and events that people you know experience in their lives. Readers of realistic fiction often find themselves drawn into the story by virtue of the parallels to their own lives. They can put themselves into the shoes of someone who is experiencing a friendship gone sour, a tragedy in the family, or a quest to follow a somewhat impossible dream. Although the parallels may not totally mirror the reader's life experiences, the connections the reader makes to a well-written realistic novel are real and memorable.

Events in a realistic novel are commonplace, situated in the present or recent past. Many focus on typical family life issues revolving around parents, children, siblings, and close friends. Contemporary realistic fiction also introduces issues of significance including suffering and unhappiness as a result of illness, tragedy, prejudice, neglect, abuse, divorce, or violence. George Eliot summed up the intent of the realistic novel

> I would not, even if I had the choice, be the clever novelist who could create a world so much better than this in which we get up in the morning to do our daily work, that you would be likely to turn a harder, colder eye on the dusty streets and the common green fields—on the real breathing men and women, who can be chilled by your indifference or injured by your prejudice.

GETTING STUDENTS HOOKED

This genre is, perhaps, the easiest and most relatable for students. They can immediately absorb much of the drama, humor, or inspiration that comes through the story. Unlike historical novels, realistic fiction invites readers into a known world. The readers do not have to find their way to places and people far removed from their everyday lives. They do not have to suspend their take on reality to accept the changed world presented in science fiction. They need not explore the imaginative fantasy world, nor begin a puzzling quest for "who did it" as experienced in mystery novels. No, the reader can just begin the journey into other lives firmly seated in their own known world. Although these may seem great advantages to enticing students to read, they may, in fact, be stumbling blocks to some readers who are hungry for sophistication, intrigue, adventure, and deep thought. Often, advanced readers begin to shy away from realistic fiction, preferring the challenges of other genres. Realistic fiction for advanced readers must be carefully chosen, ensuring the depth and complexity these readers deserve.

One great entre into realistic fiction is to help advanced students connect with stories that are relatable because the characters experience issues gifted children often face, such as expectations, perfectionism, and social isolation. Reading about characters who face issues similar to their own may be a valuable experience for these students, allowing them to recognize that they are not alone in their problems and noting possible remedies for the challenges they face.

In Chapter 13 of this book, you will find a section on developmental bibliotherapy, an option for using literature to help gifted students deal with issues they experience because of their unusual potential. The list of recommended novels in this section includes primarily realistic fiction.

REALISTIC NOVEL ELEMENTS

An effective realistic novel presents the reader with an opportunity to engage in true-to-life problem solving in thinking about some complex issue or challenge a character faces. As the story unfolds, the reader is led to consider multiple viewpoints as well as multiple options for problem resolution. Would the reader have chosen a similar path? Would some other solutions be more in keeping with the reader's world views? The effective realistic novel invites the reader into the main character's world but does not offer a "this is how you should resolve this issue" but rather a reflective look at possibilities. The overall message from the author leaves the reader recognizing that problems do have solutions and universal issues are present in everyday living.

The Setting

The setting for realistic fiction is everyday life in our society. The story typically occurs in the present time or recent past. If the story is situated in the recent past, fictionalized people are genuine to the time in which they lived. The location chosen for the story is a real place or a fictionalized place that seems real such as a family home or neighborhood, a local school, a town or city, or a particular country. The setting supports the reader's entre into the world of the main characters.

The Plot

Writers of realistic fiction provide accurate representation of everyday life and typical events, weaving stories of people that could have actually occurred. Although the stories are not true, characters resolve their issues in realistic ways. Often these issues/problems/conflicts are ones that readers can envision happening in their own lives. The situation may revolve around a personal problem, a relationship, or a contemporary social issue or event. The events are believable and the reader readily envisions the story's events, anticipating what will happen next in the quest to resolve the problem. The reader recognizes the situation as plausible, if not as a personal issue, then as something other people likely face.

The Characters

Characters in a realistic novel are fictionalized people living ordinary lives who experience a problem or a conflict and find a realistic way to resolve their issue. Generally, the author presents a main character, as well as others who are connected to the main character and involved in the details of the issue or conflict. The protagonist is an ordinary person, not a hero.

The Dialogue

The novelist uses the language natural to the characters in the story. Regional accents, slang, commonly used phrases, and specific terms related to the story are presented in the natural voices of the characters. The use of language also reflects the social class and culture of the characters.

The Point of View

As is typical in novels, the writer may choose to use first person, allowing a key character to tell the story in his or her own voice, or to use the third person, where a story is told by an outsider, using *he* or *she*, *him*, *her*, *they*, and *them*.

The Theme

The theme is a significant element in a realistic novel. The writer has a message to convey through the everyday living and struggles of the characters. In this way, the author weaves an extraordinary message into the ordinary lives depicted in the story. In realistic novels, the protagonist most often faces and overcomes a problem and becomes more self-aware and mature as a result of dealing with the issue. Sometimes the problem revolves around another person, but often it is an internal struggle. The theme may center around family, love, relationships, the value of perseverance, or triumph over adversity.

Writers of realistic fiction:
+ are excellent observers of everyday life;
+ focus their writing on things that evoke strong emotions;
+ blend imagination with realistic story details;
+ find inspiration from their own lives and stories about real people;
+ develop characters based on human struggles, large and small;
+ make their characters believable;
+ use natural conversation to reveal characters' thoughts, feelings, personalities, beliefs;
+ incorporate a human struggle and the main character's motivation to resolve the issue; and
+ present a tangible, life lesson for readers.

CHOOSING REALISTIC FICTION FOR ADVANCED READERS

In deciding on a realistic novel, select from among those that:
+ introduce relatable characters;
+ project personal problems and challenges, or social issues relatable to advanced learners;
+ offer believable situations and events;
+ ask readers to consider multiple perspectives related to the characters' challenges;
+ present a realistic view and sensitive treatment of contemporary issues;

+ encourage readers to consider their own values, dreams, challenges, and concerns; and
+ show sensitive treatment of all people without stereotyping.

REALISTIC NOVEL LIST

The following realistic novels have been chosen as good examples of outstanding use of novel elements as well as for their popularity with adolescents. Note that many realistic novels do not sugarcoat language, personal experiences, or violence or may include beliefs and actions that may be offensive to some people. Always consider the appropriateness of the entire novel for your particular class, school, and community in terms of content. You may want to seek the guidance of your librarian as you consider the selections. With thousands of excellent selections, you are sure to find books suitable for your advanced readers. A source of information about the appropriateness of content and maturity levels of books, films, and other media is http://www.commonsensemedia.org. This is an independent, nonprofit organization dedicated to providing guidance in media use with children.

+ *Out of My Mind* **by Sharon Draper (2010):** Meet Melody, an amazingly gifted young girl with a photographic memory that is constantly recording. Sadly, no one knows about Melody's gifts because she cannot speak or write. Most people, including her teachers, believe she cannot learn. Melody has been so frustrated inside, but when she discovers something that will allow her to speak, will anyone listen?
+ *Ungifted* **by Gordon Korman (2012):** Donovan is a prankster who finds himself accidentally identified as gifted and sent to the Academy for Scholastic Distinction. Although his academic achievement is pitiful at his new school, he manages to bring some of his special "gifts" to the school's programs. *Note.* A number of stereotypical views of gifted students will be found in this book. This may be a good opportunity for discussion about people's perceptions of gifted learners and the misperceptions that abound. The National Association for Gifted Children (http://www.nagc.org) website offers a short video made by gifted kids discussing myths about themselves as advanced leaners.
+ *The Outsiders* **by S. E. Hinton (1967):** This is a classic book that is still relatable to kids today. It tells the story of a boy on the fringes of regular society pitted against the privileged ones. The story offers plenty of action and lots to think about related to friendship and belonging, heroism, and family.

+ *The Fault in Our Stars* **by John Green (2012):** Sixteen-year-old Hazel has a terminal illness. She has experienced plenty of ups and downs with her illness. The focus of her life is about to change dramatically when she meets Augustus Waters at the Cancer Kid Support Group. They find they are kindred spirits ready to reach out to each other with humor and wonder about life, death, and the importance of being remembered.

+ *Jellicoe Road* **by Melina Marchetta (2006):** Taylor has not had an easy life. She was abandoned by her mother when she was 11, and now, 6 years later, the only adult Taylor trusts has disappeared. Clues Hannah left behind might lead Taylor to the truth about her past and the hopes for her future but, as leader of the boarders at her boarding school, Taylor must also prepare for the annual turf wars between the boarders, the townies, and the cadets. However, she just wants to understand the mystery of her past. (Mature themes.)

+ *The Absolutely True Diary of a Part-Time Indian* **by Sherman Alexie (2007):** This is the story of Junior, who lives on an Indian reservation, attending the reservation school, which is in poor condition. He decides to make his life better by attending the all-White school in town where he will be the only Indian (except the school's mascot). This novel is based on the author's real-life experiences.

+ *Mosquitoland* **by David Arnold (2015):** So what is Mosquitoland? That is Mim's word for Mississippi, where she has gone from Ohio to live with her dad and new stepmom. Convinced that her stepmom is trying to keep her away from her own mother, Mim decides to leave Mississippi and go back to her mom. Along the way on the long bus ride, Mim meets a number of characters, both humorous and savory, and experiences some troubling things that make her reevaluate who she is and what it means to be loyal.

+ *I'll Give You the Sun* **by Jandy Nelson (2014):** Twins Noah and Jude are both artistically talented and incredibly close. Their closeness, however, is greatly impacted by a sudden and horrible event in their lives. They become jealous of each other, especially after only Jude is accepted at a prestigious art school that Noah has had his heart set on. Barely speaking to each other, the twins begin separate lives and loves. Can anything bring them together again? The novel travels across time, being told in Noah's voice when they were 13 and in Jude's voice 3 years later, at the height of their separation. (Mature themes.)

+ *Monster* **by Walter Dean Myers (1999):** Steve Harmon is in juvenile detention and on trial for involvement in a robbery and murder. He decides to document his time in prison and the trial as a film script, like the one he had been developing in his high school film class. The novel is presented as

Steve's screenplay as well as his journal entries. Steve calls his screenplay "Monster" because that is what the prosecutor called him.

+ *Hatchet* **by Gary Paulsen (1987):** A plane crashes with 13-year-old Brian inside. He was on his way to visit his father, but now he is alone in the wilderness. His only survival tool is a hatchet, a gift from his mother. His greatest worry had been the secret he had been carrying around since his parent's divorce, but now his worries are much more immediate. How can he survive?

Realistic Novels
Student Summary Sheet

Realistic novels are stories about characters who, although fictionalized, represent people who seem real, dealing with issues people experience in everyday life.

The Setting

+ Story generally situated in contemporary times
+ Place can be real or fiction, a real-life environment that suits the characters

The Plot

+ Story revolving around issues/problems/conflicts that could really happen

The Characters

+ Fictionalized people leading fairly ordinary lives
+ Main character (protagonist) generally owns the conflict/issue/problem
+ Antagonist represents the conflict or force opposing the protagonist

The Dialogue

+ Language and speech patterns natural to the characters
+ Reflects social class and culture of the characters

The Point of View

+ Sometimes told in first person by protagonist or secondary character; uses *I*, *we*
+ Often told in third person by an outside narrator who knows only one of the characters (limited) or an all-knowing narrator (omniscient); uses *he*, *she*, *they*

The Theme

+ A significant element in realistic novels
+ Speaks to overcoming challenges and strengthening self-awareness
+ Presents extraordinary resolution of a problem within ordinary circumstances

Chapter 8

The Historical Novel

History tells us what people do; historical fiction helps us imagine how they felt.—Guy Vanderhaeghe

A historical novel, blending truth and fiction, takes the reader on a journey into the past. Unlike the historian, who seeks to uncover and report on the facts, the historical novelist seeks to tell the story behind the facts. The writer may choose to include some well-known people from the past but also invents a storyline that includes fictional characters and details of everyday life at the time. The historical novel is an emotional journey into the lives and times of the characters.

In a good historical novel, the story details ring true, providing accurate historical context for the fictional story to be told. Seeking authenticity related to the time period, a writer conducts substantial preliminary research to capture real events and specific cultural references from the time. The readers feel like they are visiting a time and place that no longer exists but was a place where real people lived long ago. In the novel, readers hear the voices of these people and learn about their perspective on the times in which they lived.

A good historical novelist stays true to the dialogue of the time, while still recognizing the need to support the understanding of the contemporary reader. The novelist knows that the language used in the novel may need to veer away from true authenticity, thus enabling today's readers to be able to conceptualize what is happening in the story. So, for example, a writer using an 1877 magazine as a historical source of information might have found this commentary about how schools might do a better job of educating young girls:

> A great many "betrothed maidens," we are sure, would be glad of such an opportunity of improving their knowledge of domestic affairs. (*Godey's Lady's Book*, 1877)

To make the language less challenging to the reader, the author might have his character say, "Young women who are engaged to be married might welcome a chance to learn more about how to manage their homes." Thus, the author maintains the ideas of the times without burdening the contemporary reader with the more authentic dialogue.

A good historical novelist does not overburden the reader with extensive details about life at the time. It is enough to ensure that the universal human condition comes through, that the theme of the story is recognizable to the reader, and that the plot is sufficient to maintain the interest of the reader without excessive details.

GETTING STUDENTS HOOKED

The best time to introduce a work of historical fiction is during a concurrent study of the past, when students' curiosity is likely aroused. Novels may be chosen in concert with the exploration of a particular historical period and/or with characters that include notable figures of the times. Knowing a bit about a certain period of time, a critical event, or an engaging historical figure generally stimulates student interest in discovering more information. At this juncture, students want to hear the stories of what happened. They are ready to learn about the "rest of the story." Reading from the perspective of someone who was on the ship, in the battle, at the protest, or going about everyday life in a strange, nontechnologically rich world introduces learners to a time in which human wants and needs were similar, but the options for solving those problems and reaching those goals were far different and limited.

HISTORICAL NOVEL ELEMENTS

The Setting

The setting is a key element in a historical novel. It sets the tone and introduces historical accuracy. The author chooses a particular time and place for the story and this backdrop influences every other element. Although the information about the time period must be accurate, the physical setting may be imaginary. Using the geography, the technology, and the economic, political and social customs, rules, and moral standards of the time, the writer moves the reader back in time to experience a plausible world in the past. The writer must be sure that details about the time period and place are accurate and authentic. Often, but not always, the setting is in a real place, enabling today's readers to wonder about and investigate the same location as it exists today. Some authors use a time travel approach, in which fictional characters of today travel back in time to experience the past, often focused on major historical events.

The Plot

Storylines for historical novels often follow linkages to well-documented events that happened at the selected time, or fictional events developed to fit the storyline. The story itself must be as believable as possible, as if it could have actually happened. Historical fiction is an effective mix of real and historically accurate events that bring believability to the story.

The plot involves a conflict, a problem, or an issue that may be personal to one character but is often incorporated into the larger issues in the society of the time.

The Characters

People developed as characters in historical novels are generally one of two types. The novelist may introduce actual historical figures (Thomas Jefferson, Martin Luther King) who were key to the plot but also include fictionalized characters, or the writer may use all fictionalized characters true to the time period. Often historical novels are a blend of both types of characterization. The true test is that the characters could have lived in the historical time and place.

The Dialogue

Dialogue is a tricky thing for the writer of historical fiction. When you select a book to read, you generally choose one that is in your language. If you have studied a foreign language, you recognize how difficult it is at first to read passages in the alternate language, constantly trying to follow the events while your mind is also in the throws of translations. That is the same issue experienced to some degree by readers of historical novels. They want to understand the story without having to do machinations in their heads to unravel what the words mean. This challenge for the writer is to modify the true dialogue of the times to enable readers to "get it" quickly and to allow the story to flow while being true to the times. The author must decide to what extent the use of historic words and phrases can be incorporated into the story without hampering readability. Certainly some words and phrases, as well as speech styles, will be necessary to create a suitable replication of the lives and times of the speakers. The effective author uses whatever it takes to make you, the reader, feel like you are there, experiencing this historical time.

The Point of View

The historical novel may be written in first person, enabling the reader to hear a voice from the past telling the story. Stories written in the first person are appealing to readers as they come to know the speaker and then see what is happening through the eyes of this storyteller. This is often a comfortable place for readers of historical fiction to begin, helping them to realize that this is not a book of "facts" but rather a look at the past as if someone were sitting beside them telling a story.

Most historical novels are written in the third person narrative, either limited, where the storyteller explains the events and feeling through only one character's eyes or all-knowing, where the narrator knows everyone's thoughts and actions.

The Theme

Universal themes transcend time, but the theme of a historical novel usually connects to the historical context of the novel. Quite often themes address social and political issues present in the era of the novel. For example, issues of conflict, interactions of different cultures, and changes in social and political systems are topics frequently incorporated into universal themes for historical novels.

Writers of historical fiction:
+ learn lots about a period and the social customs,
+ search for historical authenticity,
+ use important historical details,
+ develop images to transport readers to a different time,
+ weave the customs and manners of the time into the actions of the characters,
+ use foreshadowing or clues to invite the reader's curiosity,
+ mix authentic details with fictional accounts, and
+ provide characters with issues connected to the period in history.

CHOOSING HISTORICAL NOVELS FOR ADVANCED READERS

Historical novels are well suited to integration with the social studies curriculum. Time periods and people unknown to your students become more accessible to them. Historical novels also help direct your students to a deeper understanding of history as a written interpretation of what actually occurred in the past. By developing hypotheses and conducting research into the past, historians are, in fact, telling a story.

Historical fiction offers students:

+ accurate historical details based on historical research;
+ stories that satisfy their curiosity;
+ personalized connections with and understanding of the past as readers relate to the lives and times of the storyline;
+ reinforcement of knowledge related to important historical people and events;
+ pathways that connect the past with the present;
+ emotional connections to the narrative;
+ insight into the daily lives of the people;
+ descriptive details of everyday life not accessible in history books;
+ retellings of what happened using the voices of the characters;
+ greater conceptualization of events, cultures, and people; and
+ a view of the human complexities behind the historical facts.

HISTORICAL NOVELS LIST

The following historical novels have been chosen as good examples of outstanding use of novel elements as well as for their popularity with adolescents. Note that many historical novels do not sugarcoat language, personal experiences, or violence or may include beliefs and actions that may be offensive to some people. Always consider the appropriateness of the entire novel for your particular class, school, and community in terms of content. You may want to seek the guidance of your librarian as you consider the selections. With thousands of excellent selections, you are sure to find books quite suitable for your advanced readers. A source of information about the appropriateness of content and maturity levels of books, films, and other media is http://www.commonsensemedia.org. This is an independent, nonprofit organization dedicated to providing guidance in media use with children.

+ ***Iron Thunder: The Battle Between the Monitor and the Merrimac* by Avi (2007):** Living in Brooklyn, NY, Tom is a 13-year-old who has lost his father during the War Between the States. Seeking to help support his family, he finds a job in an ironworks where the *Monitor*, a ship made of iron, is being made. Tom learns that this ship is going to help fight the Union battle. Serving as an assistant to Captain Ericsson, the ship's inventor, Tom becomes the target of dangerous spies who offer him money for information about the ship.

+ ***North by Night: A Story of the Underground Railroad* by Katherine Ayres (1998):** Lucy Spencer's home is serving as a stop on the Underground Railroad in 1851, helping fugitive slaves escape to Canada. Her family is willing to help in spite of dangers to themselves. When she is asked to help the widow Mercer with a family of runaway slaves hiding in her attic, Lucy does so very willingly. As she becomes more connected to this family, she faces a new challenge when she is asked to leave her home and family behind.

+ ***Bull Run* by Paul Fleischman (1993):** This story tells of the first major battle of the Civil War. This unique novel offers multiple points of view, telling the story through 16 different voices including a soldier, a civilian, a slave, a freeman, people of different ages, and both Yankee and Confederate supporters.

+ ***Catch You Later, Traitor* by Avi (2015):** Pete, living in a middle-class family in Brooklyn, is surprised by his teacher's accusation of his father as a communist. The teacher supports the other students as they and their families begin to stay away from Pete and his family. When the FBI comes to call, Pete worries about what might be behind the accusation and sets out to find the truth, using his best detective skills.

+ ***Rebel Queen* by Michelle Moran (2015):** In this story of resistance to the English takeover of India, Queen Lakshmi of Jhansi is introduced through the eyes of her female guard, Sita. Sita's role as part of the Queen's band of female guards, the Dhurga Dai, reveals the politics of the time and the heroics of Queen Lakshmi and her female warriors on the battlefield in 1878.

+ ***Far as the Eye Can See* by Robert Bausch (2014):** Set in the American West in 1876, the story unfolds with the anticipation of a major confrontation between Indian tribes and the U.S. Army. An Army scout, Bobby Hale is on a search for a missing woman when he realizes that he has inadvertently killed Indians who were on a peace mission. Now he must run from both the Indians and the U.S. Cavalry.

+ ***Girl in Blue* by Ann Rinaldi (2001):** The Civil War rages and 16-year-old Sara Louisa decides to escape from being forced into marriage and join the excitement of the battlefield. She disguises herself as a boy and joins the 2nd Michigan Infantry. Later discovery as a girl ends her soldiering career but not her efforts in the war. She eventually works as a spy for Allan Pinkerton's fledgling Secret Service.

+ ***The Watsons Go to Birmingham—1963* by Christopher Paul Curtis (1995):** A Michigan family travels to Alabama, experiencing the humiliations of segregation, the joys of family, and the horror of the bombing of the 16th Street Baptist Church.

+ *Pompeii* **by Robert Harris (2003):** Set in the Roman Empire, the story tells of a young engineer who works on the aqueducts that supply the water for the town. He discovers sulfur in the water supply south of town on the slopes of Mt. Vesuvius. Searching for the cause, he and thousands are caught in an eruption of the volcano.

+ *Under a Painted Sky* **by Stacey Lee (2015):** In 1849, a young Chinese-American girl is suddenly caught up in a flight for her life, after her father dies and she accidentally murders a man who tried to assault her. Fleeing along the dangerous Oregon Trail, Samantha and her companion, a runaway slave, disguise themselves as boys headed for the gold rush in California.

+ *The Book Thief* **by Markus Zusak (2006):** Liesel Meminger is a poor foster girl living outside Munich, Germany. She steals from others at times, especially books. Her foster father helps her to learn to read and she shares her stolen books with her neighbors during bombing raids. Oh, and there is the small matter of the Jewish man hidden in her basement. She shares with him, too.

+ *Mila 18* **by Leon Uris (1983):** The last Jews held captive in the Warsaw ghetto rebel, holding off the Nazi army for 3 weeks. Incredible courage and determination are revealed through the eyes of a news correspondent, a scholar, a Polish cavalry officer, and others.

+ *The Kite Rider* **by Geraldine McCaughrean (2001):** As the Mongols invade China, an unlikely spy is at work. A young Chinese boy, Haoyou, is able to escape his family's poverty as a kite rider, strapped to a giant kite and flown above to spy for his masters.

Historical Novels
Student Summary Sheet

Historical novels are narratives in which the plot is set in the past. Characters in historical novels are fictionalized persons and/or notable historic figures authentically presented as living within the selected historical time period.

The Setting

+ The most important story element
+ Story written in a time 50 or more years ago
+ Geographic location often selected for connection to significant historical events

The Plot

+ Story well connected to social, political, and economic patterns of the time

The Characters

+ Fictionalized characters who might have lived in this setting
+ May include notable historic figures

The Dialogue

+ Speech patterns typical for the time and place
+ Archaic language may be adapted for ease of reading

The Point of View

+ Sometimes told in first person by protagonist or secondary character; uses *I*, *we*
+ Often told in third person by an outside narrator who knows only one of the characters (limited) or an all-knowing narrator (omniscient); uses *he*, *she*, *they*

The Theme

+ Often related to the political or social issues of the time
+ Universal message also relevant to contemporary readers

Quotes About Historical Fiction

History is a cyclic poem written by Time upon the memories of man.

—Percy Bysshe Shelley

If you want to understand today, you have to search yesterday.

—Pearl S. Buck

Mankind are so much the same, in all times and places, that history informs us of nothing new or strange in this particular. Its chief use is only to discover the constant and universal principles of human nature.

—David Hume

Historical novels are, without question, the best way of teaching history, for they offer the human stores behind the events and leave the reader with a desire to know more.

—Louis L'Amour

The best moments in reading are when you come across something—a thought, a feeling, a way of looking at things—which you had thought special and particular to you. And now, here it is, set down by someone else, a person you have never met, someone even who is long dead. And it is as if a hand has come out, and taken yours.

—Alan Bennett

Until lions have their historians, tales of the hunt shall always glorify the hunters.

—African Proverb

Chapter 9

The Mystery Novel

The most beautiful thing we can experience is the mysterious. It is the source of all true art and science.—Albert Einstein

Mystery novels may present a crime to solve or a puzzling situation. The intrigue may be physical or psychological, full of action and adventure, or mind-bending and perplexing entanglement. Some mystery novels may follow a path of logical thinking while others offer twists and turns and "I never saw that coming" endings.

What all mysteries have in common is a confounding situation that requires resolution. Quite often the situation is a crime that must be solved or a matter of political intrigue or deception.

Some writers of mystery novels enjoy having the reader play along with them, inserting clues along the way to entice the reader, and encouraging logical thinking to solve the mystery. Some mystery writers enjoy offering readers suspenseful, thrilling experiences that do not follow a straight path of clues. When well-written, both types of novels appeal to most gifted readers because of the intellectual challenges they present.

Mysteries generally have predictable structures, allowing the plot to assume the primary role while characters are secondary. In detective mysteries, there is one skillful crime solver who dominates the scene and is usually the one who uncovers parts of the puzzle in a progression leading to a reveal and resolution of the crime at the end of the novel. Other mysteries may offer a series of actions that are not orderly but move haphazardly toward the resolution of the puzzle or there may be a variation on the two approaches to telling a mystery tale.

The most significant and unique teaching opportunity through the use of mystery novels is in the area of logical thinking and reasoning with evidence. Mysteries are powerful ways to enhance active engagement with the printed word as well as promote the development of critical thinking.

Students enjoy the gaming aspect of solving a mystery and have tremendous motivation to think early and often, attempting to outwit other readers as well as the writer!

GETTING STUDENTS HOOKED

Students may find the predictable structure of the detective mystery enjoyable and will begin each novel with the knowledge that they, too, can solve this mystery and may be able to do so in short order using logic and sound reasoning. Other students may be put off by the "formulated" and predictable way the story is conveyed. They may soon tire of these types of novels and may seek the more exploratory, less structured style of other mystery writers. The plots in these more complex novels open possibilities regarding the content of the mystery, the context of the mystery, and the manner in which the puzzle solution is revealed. In either case the plot opens up the mind of the students as they begin to question the motives of all characters, seek patterns in the events as they unfold, and continually wonder what happened and what will be revealed through a careful reading. Readers of mysteries are significantly more actively engaged in the text than in some other genres where the reader is more reactive than partnering with the writer in solving the puzzle, whatever it may be.

Once your students determine the fundamentals of the puzzling situation, they are usually totally hooked and simply must finish reading the novel for the unraveling of the mystery. A good way to start off introducing students to mystery novels is to select one and read just the sections that establish the puzzle. Then allow them to begin the full reading of the novel. Another way to introduce mysteries is to offer introductions to several novels as headlines such as "Investigators Consider Two Key Suspects: The School Principal and the Dark and Stormy Night."

You may also want to introduce your students to logic puzzles to practice following the logic behind a set of clues in the solution of a mystery.

MYSTERY NOVEL ELEMENTS

The Setting

In the early and highly popular mystery novels written by Sir Arthur Conan Doyle, the reader follows Sherlock Holmes as the crime solver detective. The setting for the novel was closed in the sense of being a particular place and time, providing a narrow scope of possible events and guilty parties. This closed setting has been used in a great many mystery novels. The crime might have occurred in an old abandoned building, on a ship, or on a train. Some mysteries are situated on holidays or in a local shop, bank, or professional office building. These classic mystery novels enable a straightforward investigation of the crime scene and possible suspects.

Although these rather structured mystery novels continue in popularity, another quite expansive approach to situating the mystery has now found a solid place in American literature. Consider all the crime and detective shows that are highly popular on television and you can begin to recognize the extended possibilities for time and place in more contemporary mysteries. Today's mystery writers allow their imaginations and modern technological crime-solving tools to take them anywhere around the globe.

The Plot

The plot of a mystery generally begins with an incident or the discovery of something strange, then uses suspense to draw the reader into the story. It is the most essential element of a mystery novel. The plot presents the mystery that is the central reason for the story. It may be a crime, a problem, a puzzle, a secret, or an unexplained event. Key to the storyline is the element of mystery, intrigue, and suspense. The reader readily engages with the text to discover what will happen or what clues will be revealed next.

The Characters

In many mysteries, the reader will find a dichotomy: the detective versus the hunted perpetrator. Although the guilty party or the puzzling situation's resolution may not be revealed until near the end of the novel, the guilty party nonetheless has been a known and fairly prominent character throughout the story. Secondary characters are used to round out the storyline and allow some distractions from the actual guilty party. For most of the story, all characters are suspects.

The protagonist (detective) works to solve the mystery and often finds him- or herself in danger. Each suspect and his or her motives are examined in the story. Dramatic tension is heightened with foreshadowing, plot twists, and different motives being offered. The detective will examine all clues, motives, and alibis to find the guilty person.

The Dialogue

The novelist's use of language in mysteries should be appropriate to the time and place. Regional accents, colloquialisms, and specific terms related to the story are presented as "natural" to the story. In murder mysteries, some typical phrases become part of the possible dialogue like "It was a dark and stormy night . . . "

The Point of View

As is typical in novels, the writer may choose to use first person, allowing a key character to tell the story in his or her own voice, or to use the third person, where the storyteller reveals what is known by one character. If the author uses the all-knowing, omniscient point of view, the storyteller knows everything and reveals it to support the unfolding of the clues toward the resolution of the mystery.

The Theme

The most typical theme is "Crime doesn't pay," although not all mysteries are stories of crimes. In that case, underlying themes may include topics related to class differences, social privilege, family relationships, love, heroes, and heroines. Themes are often connected to human struggles and efforts to reach out and help another person or, alternatively, jealousy and the weaknesses in human relationships. Some contemporary crime mysteries involve the value of neighbors and human connections as an ordinary person becomes the hero in solving a small-town crime.

Writers of mystery novels:
+   develop the problem or crime as the central piece;
+   build the crime first and map clues out backward;
+   make their sleuth an interesting, often quirky character;
+   introduce only believable crimes with logical solutions;
+   offer clues to the reader, including at least one red herring;
+   provide multiple suspects;
+   keep the solution a secret/mystery until the end of the novel; and
+   share many details to create suspense.

CHOOSING MYSTERY NOVELS

The following mystery novels have been chosen as good examples of outstanding use of novel elements as well as for their popularity with adolescents. Note that many mystery novels do not sugarcoat language, personal experiences, or violence or may include beliefs and actions that may be offensive to some people. Always consider the appropriateness of the entire novel for your particular class, school, and community in terms of content. You may want to seek the guidance of your librarian as you consider the selections. With thousands of excellent selections, you are sure to find books quite suitable for your advanced readers. A source of information about the appropriateness of content and maturity levels of books, films, and other media is http://www.commonsensemedia.org. This is an independent, nonprofit organization dedicated to providing guidance in media use with children.

+ *Tokyo Heist* **by Diana Renn (2012):** Violet and her friend Reika are somehow mixed up with a missing Van Gogh painting. The Yakuza, an organized crime syndicate, are on the trail of the painting, threatening art dealers and anyone else who stands in their way.

+ *Paper Towns* **by John Green (2008):** Quentin knows his friend Margo is up to something when she comes to him in the middle of the night, asking him to come with her as she plots a revenge campaign. In the morning, Quentin finds that Margo is missing, but Quentin finds clues meant for him. As he follows them, he wonders if he really knows Margo at all.

+ *The Naturals* **by Jennifer Lynn Barnes (2013):** Cassie is a teenager with an exceptional ability: She can read people like a book. One day, the FBI comes to recruit her for a special classified program using exceptional teenagers to help them solve cold cases.

+ *The Westing Game* **by Ellen Raskin (1978):** An eccentric millionaire is dead and 16 people are gathered for the reading of the will. The mysterious heirs are divided into eight pairs and each pair receives a different set of clues. The pairs are challenged to solve the mystery of the murder of Sam Westing and thus receive the entire $200 million estate.

+ *I Am the Messenger* **by Markus Zusak (2002):** Ed Kennedy is an underage cab driver without a future and hopelessly in love with his friend Audrey. His life is boring and routine until he inadvertently becomes a hero, stopping a bank robbery. And then the first ace arrives in the mail with a coded message. That's when Ed becomes the messenger. Each clue sends him on another mission where he helps or hurts people along the way. He makes his way through until only one question remains: Who is behind Ed's missions?

+ *Heist Society* **by Ally Carter (2010):** Katarina has left the family business (thieving) and conned her way into a boarding school but leaving "the life" is harder than she thought. She is pulled back in when her father becomes the prime suspect for stolen paintings. In order to save her father, Kat needs to find the paintings and steal them back.

+ *Swindle* **by Gordon Korman (2008):** Griffin Bing has been swindled out of his best baseball card by a mean collector named Swindle. Griffin will stop at nothing to get his card back, so he puts together a team of friends to help get past the security system and guard dog as they seek to uncover the secret hiding place and retrieve the valuable card.

+ *We Were Liars* **by E. Lockhart (2014):** Members of the wealthy Sinclair family and their friends spend each summer on their private island off Cape Cod. The summer Cadence turns 15, she suffers a strange accident followed by amnesia and severe headaches. She just cannot seem to remember what happened. One summer seems to be a blur for Cadence. What is the mysterious secret of that fateful summer? And who were the liars? (Mature topics.)

+ *The Mysterious Benedict Society* **by Trenton Lee Stewart (2007):** Reynie Muldoon, an 11-year-old orphan, responds to an ad recruiting "gifted children looking for special opportunities." He is directed to compete in a series of challenging and creative tasks that result in he and three other children becoming the Mysterious Benedict Society. Mr. Benedict sends the group to a remote boarding school where they are to learn more about stopping an evil plot to take over the world.

+ *The Silence of Murder* **by Dandi Daley Mackall (2011):** Hope finds it incredible that her older brother Jeremy has been accused of killing the local baseball coach. Jeremy has not spoken in years, so he is unable to explain why the baseball bat has his blood on it. Believing in Jeremy's innocence, Hope is determined to prove him innocent.

Mystery Novels
Student Summary Sheet

Mystery novels are stories about crimes or puzzling situations that require resolution.

The Setting

+ Story may be situated in any time and place
+ Traditional mysteries have "closed" settings that limit the scope of suspects and events
+ Settings for contemporary mysteries are more broadly defined

The Plot

+ The most significant element of a mystery novel
+ Always incorporates a crime or puzzling situation or event

The Characters

+ Often the hunted and the hunter, detective and perpetrator in crime stories
+ Protagonist as typical mystery solver of a problem, secret, or unexplained event
+ Other major characters, suspects, or witnesses may bring forth clues

The Dialogue

+ Language and speech patterns natural to the characters
+ Reflects social class and culture of the characters

The Point of View

+ Sometimes told in first person by protagonist or secondary character; uses *I, we*
+ Often told in third person by narrator not a part of the story; uses *he, she, they*

The Theme

+ Often connected to class differences, family relations, human struggles

Chapter 10

The Science Fiction Novel

Science fiction writers foresee the inevitable, and although problems and catastrophes may be inevitable, solutions are not.—Isaac Asimov

Science fiction offers imaginative stories incorporating scientific theories. What is possible? What might happen in some future reality? The writer of science fiction blends present-day reality with possibilities that do not yet exist and, indeed, may never exist. The novelist situates characters in an ambiguous and generally complex world where they struggle with this new reality.

Science fiction generally appeals to readers who love complexity, enjoy conceptualizing, and appreciate the escapist, independent thinking required to suspend the present for a view of the future. Readers experience everyday as it might differ beyond their lifetimes. Change is inevitable and the science fiction novelist embraces that concept and offers a view of true scientific concepts with a twist that provides a "this could really happen" experience for the reader.

Blending the reading of science fiction with school topics in science not only helps students to solidify current scientific theories but also enables them to embrace science as a realm of possibilities, some of which may happen in their lifetimes, some because of their life's work.

The mark of a good science fiction writer is the ability to bridge science and real life without overwhelming the reader. The mark of a good reader of science fiction is the ability to suspend an in-depth analysis of the unusual ideas being presented ("Could that really happen? Oh, that is not accurate. I know this area of physics and this theory is way off base.") to allow the story to unfold as the primary experience. Although science is woven into the story, it takes a secondary place in the novel, allowing the emotional story to be the star.

GETTING STUDENTS HOOKED

Sometimes students shun science fiction as too strange, too deep, or just not real enough for them. You may need to offer some enticement to move students' attitudes toward this genre. Students may be fearful that they will not understand the science concepts that are woven into the story. Boys tend to be more interested in science fiction than girls, although there is likely a science fiction story for every taste. Stories range from those with aliens and space warfare to altered habitats and body modifications.

Students may be less familiar with classic science fiction novels and so a good way to start is to begin a read aloud such as one of the vignettes about the colonization of Mars from Ray Bradbury's *The Martian Chronicles*. Written in 1950, these fairly brief and somewhat interconnected short stories were originally written in the 1940s by Bradbury for a science fiction magazine series. They chronicle the fleeing of humans from a troubled and eventually atomically devastated Earth and the humans' encounters with the Martians. These stories make a good introduction to the elements of a science fiction novel as well as introduce students to the lasting qualities of good literature.

Another way to get students involved in science fiction is to select a novel related to your current science content. As students expand their understanding of a particular science topic and become more curious about what it entails, they may be more interested in a story that explores future possibilities related to that content. Several science fiction anthologies are available containing short stories that may appeal to your students. These include:

+ *I Left My Sneakers in Dimension X* by Bruce Coville, and
+ *Bruce Coville's Strange Worlds*.

You may want to offer a read aloud from the beginning of a science fiction novel. You might even provide a readers' theater with several students taking on the parts of the characters introduced in the first part of the story. A good source for ready-made readers' theater scripts is *Science Fiction Readers Theatre* by Anthony Fredericks. The book contains 20 scripts that offer students stories with creative roles of explorers, discoverers, scientists, and aliens.

Sometimes just reading and reimagining stories from random science fiction novels may stimulate motivation. This may be enough to begin a student's journey into this genre. The Novel Approach will also help your reluctant science fiction readers as they gain interest in the story through the regular discussions with other students who bring more enthusiasm for the genre.

ELEMENTS IN SCIENCE FICTION NOVELS

The Setting

In a science fiction novel, the setting can be anywhere in the world, including outer space. It may incorporate parallel worlds. Although many people's image of science fiction includes aliens and strange creatures, the majority of quality science fiction novels are situated on Earth, quite often in the future. Altered environments or totally new habitats may be found. Humans may travel to other planets or travel in time as in novels of alternate histories.

The Plot

A science fiction novel always involves some change in the world as we know it that is explained by science or technology. Such changes allow the author to invent a new world of possibilities in what might otherwise have been a realistic novel. Humans live in this altered state and may wrestle with personal problems, relationships, political structures, future life, travel, robots and other new technologies, space travel or time travel, superpowers, alien or altered beings, and impending disasters such as an alien invasion, a natural disaster, or nuclear war.

Quite popular at the moment among young adolescents are dystopian novels, those that present a future world in which disaster reigns in the form of violence, disease, and/or oppression. Often the stories show a world where humans are oppressed and controlled, supposedly for the sake of the development of a perfect society. Dystopian novels are a subgenre of science fiction. Generally, science fiction stories project a future within the realm of scientific possibilities yet unseen, but not necessarily negative.

The Characters

Characters in a science fiction novel are fictionalized people or creatures developed to fit the plot. Science fiction does not generally include scientists as key characters in the story although a main character may possess a great deal of scientific or technological knowledge. Heroes and villains are typical characters but the effective author seeks to ensure that they have relatable human characteristics. Individuals, even aliens, have personalities that are familiar even though their existence and the world in which they live may be strange. Most characters in science fiction are not typical, everyday people such as bankers, tradesmen, and lawyers and so the personalities of the characters overshadows typical roles they might play in today's world. They live in an unknown world but must be relatable because of their individuality.

The Dialogue

The novelist's use of language in science fiction is that which is appropriate to the time and place. Regional accents, colloquialisms, and specific terms are presented as "natural" to the story, although the author, because of the unreal setting of the novel, may imagine and present patterns of speech, words, and phrases that may be unfamiliar in today's world. Aliens and strange creatures may use a different type of dialect, like a new "foreign language." Science fiction characters often use specific scientific and technical terms.

The Point of View

As is typical in novels, the writer may choose to use first person, allowing a key character to tell the story in his or her own voice, or to use the third person, where a story is told by an outsider, using he, she, him, her, they, and them.

The Theme

Science fiction themes often address the quest for a perfect society. The issues of good and evil, power, political structures, and technology are often chosen as topics for the author's message.

> Writers of science fiction:
> + create imaginary worlds in detail,
> + base their ideas on actual science,
> + are familiar with scientific principles,
> + require readers to suspend belief to show them a new reality,
> + use "what if" as central to the plot,
> + add details to support the plot but do not overdo the science,
> + use logic more than fantasy, and
> + make the new reality believable enough for readers to see the possibilities.

SCIENCE FICTION NOVELS LIST

The following science fiction novels have been chosen as good examples of outstanding use of novel elements as well as for their popularity with adolescents. Note that many science fiction novels do not sugarcoat language, personal experiences, or violence or may include beliefs and actions that may be offensive to some people. Always consider the appropriateness of the entire novel for your particular class, school, and community in terms of content. You may want to seek the guidance of your librarian as you consider the selections. With thousands of excellent selections, you are sure to find books quite suitable for your advanced readers. A source of information about the appropriateness of content and maturity levels of books, films, and other media is http://www.commonsensemedia.org. This is an independent, nonprofit organization dedicated to providing guidance in media use with children.

+ *Fahrenheit 451* **by Ray Bradbury (1951):** In this future American world, books are banned and firemen are charged with burning books. Most people just mindlessly continue their lives, watching TV and shunning anyone who secretly keeps books. Montag, a fireman, wonders why some people will even sacrifice their lives to secretly keep books.

+ *Cinder* **by Marissa Meyer (2012):** In the futuristic New Beijing, new empires have been formed and the moon has been colonized. Here Linh Cinder lives as a cyborg, working as an engineer. Cinder meets Prince Kai when he seeks her help in fixing his android. When a plague attacks Cinder's stepsister, she is accused by her stepmother of causing her illness. When her stepmother volunteers Cinder for plague research, scientists uncover Cinder's immunities and her unique makeup. Meanwhile, Prince Kai is seeking to thwart the intergalactic struggle for power. Of course, there is a ball where secrets are discovered and the fate of the Earth hinges on Cinder, who must uncover secrets in her past to protect her world's future.

+ *The Maze Runner* **by James Dashner (2009):** Thomas wakes up in an elevator with no memories except his own name. He is quickly transported to a world of about 60 teenage boys living in a completely enclosed self-sustaining environment. Thomas joins the boys in unsuccessful attempts to escape through the maze that surrounds their living space. But then a girl arrives with a note and things in their world suddenly begin to change—and not for the better.

+ *The Testing* **by Joelle Charbonneau (2013):** Sixteen-year-old Malencia Vale is about to graduate, but all she can think about is whether she will be selected for the Testing, a program to select outstanding candidates for the University, where they will be trained to become leaders in revitalizing their post-war civilization. Her father has dim memories of horrible experiences with the Testing, but nothing can prepare Cia for what is to come: The Testing is full of mental and physical trials, double-crossing, and terror that eventually eliminates 80% of the candidates.

+ ***Divergent* by Veronica Roth (2011):** In a dystopian world situated in a futuristic Chicago, Beatrice must choose between staying with her family or leaving to be her true self. It will soon be time for her decision as all 16-year-olds must choose one of five factions, Candor (the honest), Abnegation (the selfless), Dauntless (the brave), Amity (the peaceful), and Erudite (the intelligent) to belong to for the rest of their lives. When Beatrice is tested for her strengths, it is discovered that she is Divergent—that she doesn't "fit" into any one faction, a characteristic considered very dangerous.

+ ***The Eye of Minds* by James Dashner (2013):** Michael spends so much time on the VirtNet as a gamer that he has been recognized by the government as a very talented hacker in the virtual reality world, where the line between what's real and what's not is blurred. In need of assistance in catching a master hacker, the government asks Michael to accept the challenge, moving from the virtual world into the reality of cyberterrorists. Can Michael help make the virtual world safe again?

+ ***The House of the Scorpion* by Nancy Farmer (2002):** Matteo was harvested, not born. Developed in a petri dish, many consider him a monster, except for El Patron who loves Matt and saves him from the fate of other cloned children. He tries to escape from those who threaten him, including El Patron's power-hungry family and the dangerous army of bodyguards. A sequel to this award-winning book is *The Lord of Opium* (2013).

+ ***The Lost Planet* by Rachel Searles (2014):** In this space adventure, Chase Garrety wakes up in a place he does not recognize, a blaster wound to the back of his head, and no memory of his past. He only knows he has a message, "Guide the star." When he and his new companion Parker witness an attack on their planet, they fear war has begun.

+ ***Parasite Pig* by William Sleator (2002):** Ready for a man-eating crab? How about a 7-foot washer woman? Barney is working after school to earn money for the damages he caused to his parents' beach house in a battle with aliens. Really, he cannot seem to get them to believe that aliens caused the damage. Too bad they don't know Barney actually saved the world by outsmarting these strange visitors who play a strange game called Interstellar Pig.

+ ***Feed* by M.T. Anderson (2002):** When Titus and his friends return from a fun trip to the moon, they discover that their feeds, the inner electronic workings implanted into their brains, have been hacked. While in the hospital to repair his malfunctioning systems, Titus meets Violet, a very intelligent girl who is planning to fight the feed and its ability control human thoughts and desires.

+ *A Wrinkle in Time* **by Madeleine L'Engle (1962):** Meg's father, a scientist who has been engaged in top-secret work for the government on the tesseract (a wrinkle in time), has disappeared. Fortunately for the family, help comes in the guise of three strange old ladies who help Meg, her very gifted brother Charles, and their friend Calvin learn what life is like on other worlds and how they can bring Meg's father home.

Science Fiction
Student Summary Sheet

Science fiction combines reality with elements based on science that do not currently exist and/or may never exist.

The Setting

+ Anywhere in the real world including outer space
+ Current time of the writing or some future time

The Plot

+ Always includes some change in the world as we know it
+ Always incorporates science and/or technology that can explain some imaginative change in people, places, or things

The Characters

+ Fictionalized people existing in the real world
+ Robots or other scientifically plausible (think mutant) creatures may be included

The Dialogue

+ Basic speech patterns and language typical for the time and place
+ Invented forms of dialogue for imaginary creatures and/or robots

The Point of View

+ May be told in third person by storyteller; uses *he*, *she*, *they*
+ May be told in first person by protagonist or secondary character; uses *I*, *we*

The Theme

+ Frequent use of the past and future state of the universe, alien beings, artificial intelligence, bio-tech, unusual habitats, technology, space travel, and new world political structures

Quotes About Science Fiction

I think science fiction helps us think about possibilities, to speculate—it helps us look at our society from a different perspective. It lets us look at our mores, using science as the backdrop, as the game changer.

—*Mae Jemison, astronaut*

For bedtime reading, I usually curl up with a good monograph on quantum physics or string theory, my specialty. But since I was a child, I have been fascinated by science fiction. My all-time favorite is The Foundation Trilogy, by Isaac Asimov.

—*Michio Kaku, physicist*

I think a lot of people are frightened of technology and frightened of change, and the way to deal with something you're frightened of is to make fun of it. That's why science fiction fans are dismissed as geeks and nerds.

—*Iain Banks, writer*

Science fiction, outside of poetry, is the only literary field which has no limits, no parameters whatsoever.

—*Theodore Sturgeon, writer*

Change is the principal feature of our age and literature should explore how people deal with it. The best science fiction does that, head on.

—*David Brin*

I'm fond of science fiction. But not all science fiction. I like science fiction where there's a scientific lesson, for example—when the science fiction book changes one thing but leaves the rest of science intact and explores the consequences of that. That's actually very valuable.

—*Richard Dawkins, scientist*

Chapter 11

The Fantasy Novel

I like nonsense, it wakes up the brain cells. Fantasy is a necessary ingredient in living.—Dr. Seuss

Enter a world of pure imagination and you have found the space in which fantasy novels are created. There are no rules for fantasy novels. Although many follow patterns that include beginnings like "Once upon a time . . . " or include characters borrowed from mythology, no such requirements exist for a fantasy novel. Authors of fantasy are free to invent new forms, patterns, and styles of storytelling.

Evidence of the lasting impression of fantasy novels on our modern world can be found in a place called The Wizarding World of Harry Potter, a theme park at Universal Studios in Florida, as well as the series of Harry Potter movies. Such tributes to the works of J. K. Rowling underline the popularity of the genre. Other highly popular novelists in the fantasy world include J. R. R. Tolkien, author of *The Hobbit* and *The Lord of the Rings*, and C. S. Lewis, who wrote The Chronicles of Narnia series.

Entering the world of the author's imagination, the reader of a fantasy novel is invited into a place where everything is possible. Characters may have super powers; animals may assume human traits; normal events suddenly take on an extraordinary air. Magic of some sort is found in every fantasy novel, directing the reader to suspend reality and enter into a different world. Such magic is used purposefully, allowing the storyline to exist. The author's inspiration often comes from folklore and mythology. The reader is generally introduced to supernatural phenomena with no basis in science. Sometimes novels cross over and distinctions are challenging between science fiction and fantasy, but fantasy diverges from the scientific basis for the story and focuses more on the imaginative possibilities rather than the scientific ones. In science fiction, the author usually elaborates more on the experimental scientific possibilities rather than the social and political possibilities. Related to fantasy are horror stories or the world of the macabre. In fantasy novels, the elements are intertwined and usually no one is more significant than another.

GETTING STUDENTS HOOKED

Fantasy novels are an easy sell for most young adolescents. Many of the most popular contemporary novels are written as series and thus feed their popularity. Most of your students are familiar with the Harry Potter series, the Percy Jackson and the Olympians series, and the Twilight saga. You will find that students are often already reading these books for pleasure, so you might begin with a discussion about the current fantasy novels students are hooked on.

An alternative would be a read aloud of sections from a novel, enough to get the students interested in the story. For example, *Coraline* by Neil Gaiman is a quite chilling and creepy story, full of rich descriptions and responsive characters. This horror/fantasy may be quite familiar to your students, but Gaiman's masterful use of language makes it an enriching experience to hear it read aloud. You may choose to read a few sections of this novel and then contrast with brief passages from another fantasy novel that is of a different type, like one featuring kings, queens, and fairies.

Modern fantasy novels often incorporate teenage characters as protagonists who assume the hero/heroine roles as opposed to the knights and princesses of fairy tales. Modern fantasy fiction writing generally incorporates these elements:

+ a story that could not actually happen in our known world,
+ a realistic setting on Earth and in contemporary times,
+ the use of magical powers or superhuman abilities, and
+ characters who are believable in the context of the fantasy.

FANTASY NOVEL ELEMENTS

The Setting

The setting for fantasy novels is usually an imaginary world created just for the novel. It can, however, be a realistic world within which fantasy elements are introduced. The story frequently occurs in a medieval setting, characters have magical powers, and mythical beings often inhabit the setting of the story. Characters may start out in the real world but travel through some magical portal to a world beyond. Whatever the place and time, the setting remains a consistent backdrop for the unfolding story.

The Characters

Fantasy novels usually include some humans but also are home to gods and heroes, monsters and adventurers, wizards and witches, elves, fairies, gnomes, goblins, trolls, sprites, angels and devils, and other creatures that could not live in the known world. A fantasy novel may draw real-world characters into the fantasy setting or a world that appears to be just like the one they live in but, in fact, has odd, bizarre, and unreal characteristics.

The characters in a fantasy novel are often magical creatures, archetypal figures inspired by folklore or myths. Characters may be animals or humans or things. They may be things with magical powers or human characteristics, animals with human characteristics, real situations with fantastic creatures or characters, real people in fantastic places, characters with magical powers, or those who experience supernatural occurrences.

The Plot

In every fantasy novel, the reader will find a tale woven around the use of magic, supernatural characters, and/or fantastic elements. The storyline in a fantasy novel usually follows a typical sequence: a hero or heroine has a problem or a challenge which takes him or her and related characters on a journey, often begun through a portal where amazing adventures lead to the resolution of the problem by some magical powers. It may be a societal or personal life problem, a character's coming of age, or a hero's journey of challenge, quest, and resolution. Action in the novel often revolves around the traditional roles and stereotypes of particular characters such as the villain, the hero, the sprite, or the king.

The Dialogue

The language in fantasy novels may be stylized to match the setting. At times, characters may assume a particular pattern of speech to suit their stereotypical behavior. Often characters are everyday human beings who speak as they might within the normal context of their lives, including regional dialects, class, and status. Fantasy tales often include a great deal of repetition, clichés, and made-up words.

The Point of View

Although first person point of view may be used ("I"), it is somewhat limiting in a fantasy novel because the view of the imaginative, fantastic world would only be through the words and eyes of the main character. It is more likely that the novelist will choose an alternative but not always.

The author may choose third person limited to share a view of the story that tells the reader the story through the thoughts and feelings of one character (he, she). The third person omniscient or all-knowing point of view allows the reader to hear the story from the perspective of all the characters and their thoughts and feeling as well as all the events, for the storyteller knows all (he, she, they).

The Theme

Themes for fantasy novels encompass universal truths such as good and evil, right and wrong, happiness, loyalty, love, fear and security, and human values. Symbolism often plays a significant role in fantasy literature, often through the use of archetypal figures inspired by earlier texts or folklore. Some argue that fantasy literature and its archetypes fulfill a function for individuals and society and the messages are continually updated for current societies.

Writers of fantasy:
+ allow their imagination free reign,
+ create a whole world and imagine their characters living in it,
+ use magic as the vehicle for problem solving,
+ ensure that their form of magic works in the chosen setting,
+ use point of view thoughtfully to allow the characters to emerge,
+ do not depend on science for what happens,
+ often borrow ideas from mythology or history,
+ avoid trite phrases and clichés, and
+ use a "no limits" approach to their writing.

FANTASY NOVELS LIST

The following fantasy novels have been chosen as good examples of outstanding use of novel elements as well as for their popularity with adolescents. Note that many fantasy novels do not sugarcoat language, personal experiences, or violence or may include beliefs and actions that may be offensive to some people. Always consider the appropriateness of the entire novel for your particular class, school, and community in terms of content. You may want to seek the guidance of your librarian as you consider the selections. With thousands of excellent selections, you are sure to find books quite suitable for your advanced readers. A source of information about the appropriateness of content and maturity levels of books, films, and other media is http://www.commonsensemedia.org. This is an independent, nonprofit organization dedicated to providing guidance in media use with children.

+ *The Land of Stories: The Wishing Spell* **by Chris Colfer (2012):** What is the power in the masked man's magic potion? He can use it to turn every book it touches into a portal. Seeking out the worst villain in literature, he must be stopped! Can Alex and Conner convince the others that they are in danger? Will Goldilocks, Jack, Red Riding Hood, and Mother Goose help them?

+ *Mark of the Thief* **by Jennifer Nielsen (2015):** In ancient Rome, Nic, a slave, is forced into a cave to retrieve treasure. Inside he discovers a bulla, an amulet that belonged to Julius Caesar. This amulet has magical powers and Nic takes it for himself. Now all of Rome is looking for him and the amulet. He must keep the amulet to avoid it causing war. Who can he turn to?

+ *Eragon* **by Christopher Paolini (2003):** Eragon thinks he is meant to just be a farmhand, until he discovers he's meant to ride dragons instead. Soon, Eragon and his dragon Saphira are dragged into a battle to ensure justice can be returned to the realm.

+ *Wings of Fire: The Dragonet Prophecy* **by Tui T. Sutherland (2012):** Five young dragonets, living under a mountain, have been destined to fulfill the prophecy ending the war raging among dragon tribes. They have been raised in secret by Talons of Peace. How will they achieve their destiny? No one knows.

+ *Warriors: Omen of the Stars #1: The Fourth Apprentice* **by Erin Hunter (2009):** Jayfeather and Lionblaze are awaiting a sign that directs them to join an unknown third cat as the ones chosen to fulfill a prophecy. All of the clans are suffering from heat and drought, but can they bond together or will there be new battles?

+ *The Lost Hero* **by Rick Riordan (2010):** Jason has no memory of his previous life, but seems to be with friends as they head on a bus to the Grand Canyon. Suddenly they are attacked by storm spirits who capture their coach. Then they meet Annabeth, searching for the lost hero Percy Jackson, who takes them to a camp where they are revealed as demigods, children of gods in their Roman personae. These teens must rescue the queen of the gods or else the giant king will rise and destroy Zeus and unseat the gods.

+ *Five Kingdoms: Sky Raiders* **by Brandon Mull (2014):** Welcome to the Outskirts, a place between wakefulness and dreaming. Is it real or just imagination? When Cole Randolph set out for Halloween fun, little did he know that the spooky house he would visit would turn out to be a portal into something even creepier. Cole watches friends vanish to a place underneath the haunted house and when he goes after them, he arrives in the Outskirts. Once you go to the Outskirts, it is very hard to leave.

+ *Artemis Fowl* **by Eoin Colfer (2001):** Take a magical journey with Artemis Fowl, a very wealthy and intelligent person. Oh, and he's also a criminal mastermind. When he kidnaps a fairy, Artemis is in big time trouble. He doesn't know how dangerous these fairies are—but they're not like those in bedtime stories.

+ *The Cabinet of Wonders* **by Marie Rutkowski (2008):** Meet Petra Kronos, whose father is far away in Prague where he was commissioned by the prince to build the world's first astronomical clock. Her father is an amazing man who can move metal with his mind. But when he returns home, he is blind! The prince has stolen his eyes and is wearing them. Now it is up to Petra to find out why and figure out how to get them back. She also discovers that her father's clock has the power to destroy the world!

The Fantasy Novel
Student Summary Sheet

Fantasy novels are works of true imagination, inviting the reader to suspend reality and enter a world that cannot be. Magic and superpowers are part of the fantastic experience.

The Setting

+ An imaginary world or imaginative variations in the real world
+ Often a medieval setting
+ Setting is a backdrop for the magical events in the story
+ May include time travel

The Plot

+ Generally a quest, a journey, or a "good versus evil" story
+ Always incorporates action based on supernatural characters and events

The Characters

+ Humans and/or animals
+ Heroes, gods, monsters, wizards and witches, elves, fairies, gnomes, goblins, trolls
+ Mythical creatures

The Dialogue

+ Basic speech patterns typical for the time and place
+ Archaic language may be used
+ May include repetition, proverbs, clichés, invented words

The Point of View

+ Most often told in third person by storyteller; uses *he, she, they*
+ Sometimes told in first person by protagonist or secondary character; uses *I, we*

The Theme

+ Frequent use of good versus evil, love, friendship, patterns of life, beauty, sacrifice
+ Universal message also relevant to contemporary readers

Quotes About Fantasy

My eighth grade teacher, Mrs. Pabst, had done her master's thesis on Tolkien. She showed me how the trilogy was patterned after Norse mythology. She was also the first person to encourage me to submit stories for publication. The idea of writing a fantasy based on myths never left me, and many years later, this would lead me to write Percy Jackson.

—Rick Riordan

We don't create a fantasy world to escape reality. We create it to be able to stay.

—Lynda Barry, cartoonist

I learned years ago from Lester del Ray that the secret to writing good fantasy is to make certain it relates to what we know about our own world. Readers must be able to identify with the material in such a way that they recognize and believe the core truths of the storytelling.

—Terry Brooks

If the story is set in a universe that follows the same rules as ours, it's science fiction. If it's set in a universe that doesn't follow our rules, it's fantasy. It's the rocket ship versus the magic carpet.

—Orson Scott Card

All cartoon characters and fables must be exaggerations, caricatures. It is the very nature of fantasy and fable.

—Walt Disney

Imagination is more important than knowledge. For knowledge is limited to all we know and understand, while imagination embraces the entire world, and all there ever will be to know and understand.

—Michael Scott

Fantasy is silver and scarlet, indigo and azure, obsidian veined with gold and lapis lazuli. Reality is plywood and plastic, done up in mud brown and olive drab. Fantasy tastes of habaneros and honey, cinnamon and cloves, rare red meat and wines as sweet as summer. Reality is beans and tofu, and ashes at the end.

—George R. R. Martin

Chapter 12

The Graphic Novel

Graphic novels are actually "sequential art narratives."—James
Bucky Carter

If you have ever read a comic book, you have met a relative of the graphic novel.
Like the comic book, the graphic novel tells much of the story through the art.
Because the graphic novel is more a presentation style than a genre, this chapter
offers you a view of the characteristics of these novels rather than details on the
specifics of the common elements of novel. Graphic novels represent a variety of
genres such as historical fiction, fantasy, mystery, science fiction, realistic stories,
and even nonfiction and biographies.

Increasingly popular with adolescents, as well as adults, graphic novels represent a combination of art and narrative. You can think of graphic novels as longer
and more fully developed comic books with more complex stories. Many of the first
graphic novels repeated and extended superhero stories, similar to the old comic
books wherein the main character is known for his superpowers. Today you will
find every possible form of novel writing presented in the graphic novels.

The focus of the graphic novel is the art. Because the dialogue and narration do
not carry the storyline like they do in regular novels, the graphic novel is unique
in its presentation. The graphic art is the star. Dialogue is sparse. Narration is secondary. All combine to tell the story. The author and illustrator (sometimes the
same person, sometimes not) choose which parts of the storyline cannot be presented through the illustrations and then carefully choose as few words as possible
to round out the story. They have a unique ability to "see" the whole story in their
mind's eye.

CHARACTERISTICS OF GRAPHIC NOVELS

Plot as Linear Narrative

The graphic novel tells a sequential story depicted in frames that generally read from right to left and top to bottom as you would read a standard novel. The story is told in frames with each frame building upon the previous ones. Panels contain several frames and each panel is a scene in the story. All present a logical progression from beginning to end. Many stories contain rich and complex plots, appealing to the advanced readers who must think beyond the printed page and make connections among graphics, dialogue, and narrative lines.

Economy of Words

The author carefully chooses the dialogue offered to the reader and captures it in balloons. Spoken words are generally presented in balloons with a tail indicating the speaker. Thoughts are also presented in balloons, but they generally have a small series of bubbles at the end to designate the thinker. Captions are used sparingly to provide needed information about the scene or event. Each word is selected to move the storyline forward in concert with the graphics.

Detailed Graphics

The illustrations play the starring role in graphic novels. The use of light and dark shades, brilliant and somber colors offer the reader a sense of the mood. The careful attention to details reveals critical story elements. Figures may represent real people or they may be drawn as symbolic of a group or an idea. Some figures may be left with blank faces, offering the reader the interpretation of feelings. Others may present exaggerated expressions, revealing the character's mood. The positioning of arms, legs, and torso is often indicative of specific motions.

Special Effects

The author wants to create the entire sense of the setting and the action but does not have the use of sentences with descriptive words and phrases as a traditional novelist does. To convey more of what is happening in the story, the author often uses words expressing sound effects (e.g., pow, boom, pop, plonk, klang, aggh, crash, wham). This literary device is called *onomatopoeia* and it is often used to emphasize action that is specific, intense, and loud. Dialogue and captions, just like graphic art, may have specific color, texture, and sizes to convey mood and drama.

In a sense, graphic novels can be considered simplified complexity. What this means for your advanced readers is that this relatively unique form of storytelling can be an opportunity for you and your students to explore new possibilities in analyzing, evaluating, and creating. Unlike straightforward narrative passages, the mix of images and words requires substantial mental manipulation. This takes your students out of their regular patterns of thinking and forces them to explore new ground. Graphic novels are particularly effective in promoting inferential thinking and evidence-based judgments. In today's world, everyone is constantly bombarded with visual images. We not only see these images in every part of our lives, but we also contribute to them via social media. A new visual image is just one swipe away. And when we look at the images we have created, we are often struck by the true story they tell. Because you and your students are living in such an image-rich world, graphic novels offer you a wonderful means to promote visual literacy.

GETTING ADVANCED READERS HOOKED

Introducing your students to a graphic novel will likely be a surprise to them. They will probably not expect to see something comic-like being provided to them as their assigned reading material. Often they are hooked on traditional books and may initially push back from completing assignments related to reading a graphic novel. A good way to begin is to project a few pages from a graphic novel and allow students to complete a Think-Pair-Share activity so that they can study the graphics and words, talk it through with a partner, and then engage in a class discussion. Taking some time to do this will enable those students who are already familiar with graphic novels to share their insight as they begin to direct the discussion and then for others to participate with their own interpretations. A good place for you to start is by acquiring a copy of *Reading With Pictures: Comics That Make Kids Smarter* by Josh Elder. This book offers guidance on how to read comics that you can easily translate into ideas for reading graphic novels. You can select one of the 12 short stories included in the book to support your students' entre into reading graphic novels. Each of the stories is relatable to a content area such as language arts, science, math, and social studies. You can then assign work on graphic novels (e.g., creating a science experiment in graphic style, a brief graphic of an event in history) that integrates your reading program with other content areas. The web tool Make Beliefs Comix (http://www.makebeliefscomix.com) is a great resource for students to create their own comic. Students can develop their characters and storyline in 2, 3, or 4 panels. The website offers support and suggestions for using comics in the classroom. Type "comic strip tools" into a search engine for other options. There are many and the list is continually growing.

Many publishers are releasing graphic novel versions of popular books. If you choose to use the novel *Fahrenheit 451*, you may find the graphic novel version of this story worthwhile to incorporate into your instruction on graphic novels. Other classic novels, such as *A Wrinkle in Time*, are also presented in graphic form.

Two additional book references for you and your students are:

+ Eisner, W. (2008). *Graphic storytelling and visual narrative.* New York, NY: W.W. Norton.
+ McCloud, S. (2006). *Making comics: Storytelling secrets of comics, manga and graphic novels.* New York, NY: William Morrow.

An excellent web source for an organization promoting graphic novels in the classroom is http://www.readingwithpictures.org. The Reading With Pictures organization advocates for the use of comics/graphic novels in the classroom. It suggests that this use promotes literacy and improves educational outcomes for all students. The organization supports research into the use of graphics in education as part of their mission to provide best practices for integrating comics into the curriculum.

GRAPHIC NOVELS LIST

The following is a list of the 2015 Top Ten graphic novels for teens as selected by the Young Adult Library Services Association. A full list of great graphic novels for teens is available at its website: http://www.ala.org/yalsa/2015-great-graphic-novels-teens-top-ten.

+ *Afterlife With Archie: Escape From Riverdale* **by Roberto Aguirre-Sacasa, Illustrated by Francesco Francavilla (2014):** Archie and his fellow survivors find refuge in Veronica's mansion when a zombie outbreak occurs in Riverdale.
+ *Bad Machinery, Vol. 3: The Case of the Simple Soul* **by John Allison (2014):** Tackleford's abandoned barns begin going up in flames. Linton and Sonny investigate the case. Is it possible that a terrifying creature living under a bridge has something to do with the mystery?
+ *47 Ronin* **by Mike Richardson, Illustrated by Stan Sakai (2014):** This is the tale of the legendary Japanese group 47 Ronin and their mission to avenge their wronged master.
+ *In Real Life* **by Cory Doctorow and Jen Wang (2014):** Anda's love of gaming becomes more complicated with the discovery that not everyone plays by the rules.
+ *Ms. Marvel, Vol. 1: No Normal* **by G. Willow Wilson, Illustrated by Adrian Alphona (2014):** Kamala Khan, a young Muslim-American girl,

dealing with her desire to just be normal, discovers she has bizarre powers. How will she use her new identity as Ms. Marvel?

+ *Seconds: A Graphic Novel* **by Bryan Lee O'Malley (2014):** Katie, a talented young chef, suddenly finds her life has taken a turn for the worse. Lucky for her, a mysterious girl introduces her to the magical powers of some mushrooms that make her life better. But Katie wants it to be perfect!

+ *The Shadow Hero* **by Gene Luen Yang and Sonny Liew (2014):** Hank's mother, rescued by a superhero, decides that her son should also be a superhero. Hank at first shuns the role but eventually is inspired to call himself the Green Turtle and begins to fight crime in his neighborhood.

+ *Through the Woods* **by Emily Carroll (2014):** This is a collection of five spooky stories about terrifying events occurring in the woods.

+ *Trillium* **by Jeff Lemire (2014):** In 3797, a botanist researches a strange species on a remote space station. In 1921, An English explorer travels the dense jungles of Peru searching for the "lost Temple of the Incas." These two souls fall in love, bringing about the end of the universe.

+ *Wolf Children: Ame & Yuki* **by Mamoru Hosoda, Illustrated by Yu (2014):** Hana falls in love with a young man who is part wolf. Soon after the young couple begin family life, setting in with their two children, the father dies in an accident. Hana must find ways to parent her two werewolf children on her own.

Chapter 13

Developmental Bibliotherapy
Supporting Advanced Readers

We read to know we are not alone.—C. S. Lewis

Did you ever pick up a book and immediately connect with the main character? Did you think, "Oh, that is just like me!"? Did you quickly relate to the storyline as somehow reflecting your own life? Has a book ever moved you to change your attitude or even your actions? That kind of response to a book is at the heart of developmental bibliotherapy, the use of selected literature to help facilitate a person's growth and self-actualization.

Because your gifted learners face unique challenges in their everyday lives, bibliotherapy may be particularly helpful to them. In addition to their need for daily school experiences that inspire and intrigue them, your advanced students often require support for social and emotional issues that differ in kind or intensity from their age peers. You have probably noticed some advanced students struggling with things like friendships, perfectionism, high expectations, and extreme sensitivity. They sometimes take on the weight of the world, trying to figure out how to solve problems like hunger or discrimination and, at other times, are so self-absorbed that you worry about the depths of their inner thoughts. High levels of stress sometimes come from within and at other times from the expectations of parents and other important people in their lives.

Bibliotherapy is the use of literature to direct a reader's thinking about a personal problem or challenge as reflected in the characters and theme of a book or other literature such as poetry. You may have heard this term before as a method used in counseling and therapeutic work with children who have mental health issues such as depression, suicide ideation, or addiction. As the term is used here, however, it suggests a teaching tool you can use with advanced learners whose issues are "normal" or common for this population (see Table 4 for a list of common developmental issues for gifted learners). For this reason, this book labels it as *developmental bibliotherapy* to distinguish it from therapeutic use.

Table 4

Common Developmental Issues of Gifted Learners

Concern	Common Thoughts of Advanced Learners
Feelings of being different	Why can't I be like everyone else?
Perfectionism	What if I don't get all A's? What if I make a mistake?
Friendship	How can I make friends when my interests are not their interests?
Expectations of others	What if my parents are disappointed in me? Will my teacher think I am not really smart?
Feelings of being misunderstood, teased	Why don't people understand that I am just me, not a nerd, a geek, or a snob?
Advanced knowledge	Why does this stuff have to be so boring? I learned this years ago!
Worry, concern for world problems	What can I do? How can people just ignore this problem?

Most gifted children feel out of sync with their age peers. They often experience challenges with friendships. Their interests may not match those of others their age. They may get caught in the trap of perfectionism. Most schoolwork comes easily to them. They are frequently "on top," receiving the highest grades and the most recognition for their academic achievements. This can lead them to a constant fear of making a mistake or not being the best. You may find your gifted students using their talents to the extreme, involved in multiple projects and, as a result, feeling stressed yet unwilling to let go of anything. When the challenges get to be too much for a student, the use of developmental bibliotherapy may be one way of extending your support within being overly intrusive.

DEVELOPMENTAL BIBLIOTHERAPY
IN THE CLASSROOM

So how should you begin to support your advanced students through developmental bibliotherapy? You might begin by selecting an issue that many of your gifted students have in common. Then you can select a novel for the group that will open up conversations that help the students to recognize that they are not alone in their challenges. For example, many gifted students deal with multipotentiality and the burdens of having too many options. A novel group using a book like *If I Love You, Am I Trapped Forever?* might be just right. In this book the main character is handsome and multitalented. He worries about everyone's expectations including those of his parents, his friends, and himself.

Developmental bibliotherapy can be useful as a general support to the group in handling issues that often go along with giftedness. Blending cognitive growth with social and emotional support is a wining instructional strategy.

SELECTING BOOKS FOR DEVELOPMENTAL BIBLIOTHERAPY

You will find that realistic novels are most typically the genre where the common social and emotional issues of advanced learners are mirrored. Because such novels are generally set in present time and familiar places, it is the issues presented in these novels that offer students opportunities for envisioning others like them, confronting similar problems. As the story unfolds and the characters work through their issues, the readers can empathize, using the reading experience to consider parallel issues and potential steps forward for themselves.

Books selected for using developmental bibliotherapy with gifted readers should incorporate:

+ interesting characters displaying gifted characteristics;
+ problems, issues, or situations that are relatable to gifted students;
+ complex, challenging, thought-provoking plots;
+ rich language, sophisticated writing;
+ content at an appropriate maturity level for young adolescents; and
+ selections appropriate to the particular issues of individual students or groups.

Suggestions are included in the book list provided at the end of this chapter. Remember, bibliotherapy is not just about finding books with gifted characters, it is about finding books where the issues the characters face are reflective of the issues currently being faced by the students.

ENGAGING STUDENTS IN THE DEVELOPMENTAL BIBLIOTHERAPY PROCESS

To attain the goal of developmental bibliotherapy, the student moves through three phases of reflection.

1. **Relates to the character:** The student relates to the gifted character in the book. *Oh, I am just like (character) in some ways.*
2. **Reacts emotionally:** The student understands the character's problem and feels the emotions it causes. *Oh, I sure know how that feels.*
3. **Reflects on solutions:** The student gains new insight into the issue and sees personal applications. *I might try something new; reading this book gave me an idea.*

Using developmental bibliotherapy in conjunction with the Novel Approach requires very little change. The choice of questions should be more directly related to the issue you have chosen for the group. Questions guide students in preparing to address the issue in their discussion circle using details from the novel. The following questions can help you to guide the thinking of your advanced learners as they come to recognize characteristics in themselves mirrored in the novel's characters. As students prepare for responding to the questions in a discussion circle, they should complete the same type of recording of evidence from the novel as they do for any other novel. Being able to cite passage that helped them to respond to the questions will be important in these discussions. For each reading section, you should also include at least one question that is more related to the elements of a novel than to the discussion of emotional problem solving. The novelist's effective use of these elements, especially the novel's theme, should be discussed.

Questioning for Developmental Bibliotherapy
+ Was this novel true to life? Did you think it was believable?
+ Did you make a personal connection with any of the characters?
+ What was the big issue this character was facing?
+ Have you ever known someone who experienced this issue?
+ Have you ever faced something similar?
+ How did you feel about this issue?
+ How did the main character feel about this issue?
+ Does the main character have any special talents or strengths?
+ How did the character resolve his or her problem?
+ Who helped the character work through the problem?
+ If you were this character, what would you have done?
+ Do you have any advice for this character?
+ Do you think this is a problem many people have?
+ What were some big ideas you were left with after your reading?
+ What makes this issue a challenge?
+ Do you think the author ended the novel satisfactorily?
+ Can you identify the theme of the novel, stating it in a sentence?
+ What "take aways" did you get from this novel?

THE DISCUSSION CIRCLE

The small-group discussion might be one you choose to guide more directly to ensure the focus is maintained. Students should feel free to openly discuss their experiences and their feelings. Usually students are relieved to discuss these common issues with others who have had similar feelings. In the group, some of the students may suggest solutions that worked for them. This personalization of the discussion is the main way in which these discussions differ from those in the Novel Approach that are not targeted toward a particular group nor a particular issue addressed in the novel. Many of the Novel Approach activities are designed for students to read and reflect. Having identified a novel for the group, use the strategies for group preparation and discussion described earlier in the book as the Novel Approach.

At the end of this discussion, encourage the students to talk about ways in which reading a novel wherein the characters are particularly relatable to specific issues might be helpful to the readers. Suggest that many other novels address issues that are common for students who have concerns about things like people's expectations, being misunderstood by peers, and finding friends. You may then choose additional novels targeted at specific groups of students and/or provide lists of novels that address common issues of advanced learners so that students may also choose to take a personal journey through the selection of novels.

REFLECTIONS ON THE NOVEL

Reflection begins as students summarize their discussion of the novel, articulate the author's theme, and make connections between the issue presented in the novel and their own lives. Additional reflective activities may include:

+ **Journal entries:** Ask students to complete brief journal entries at the end of each section of the book as well as a summative reflection at the end of the novel reading. You may provide a prompt for each journal entry, asking students to consider their perspective on the focus issue as it is presented in the book as well as in their own lives.

+ **Readers' theater:** Ask small groups to take turns selecting a part of the novel to read aloud. Encourage them to choose a section wherein the characters articulate their thoughts about the problem, interact with others about the issue, or engage in activities in support of the resolution of the issue. Students should read the entire narrative and dialogue, assigning different readers for different parts.

+ **Role-play:** At the conclusion of a section of the novel, invite students to volunteer to role-play a particularly interesting encounter from the novel. You may ask them to first role-play the issue as it unfolded in the novel and then develop a role-play for a way in which they might have approached the encounter and its results in a different way. Students do not read from the novel, but improvise their own script and actions to either mirror the events from the novel or create a new scene related to the same issue.
+ **Further discussion:** Encourage students to continue reflecting on their reading and thinking about the issue through further discussions with peers, a mentor, counselor, parents, or you as their teacher.
+ **Learning activities:** Learning activity sheets are included in this chapter to promote applicable reflections. You may select ones that seem most appropriate for the novel selected for discussion. Because writing activities are particularly supportive of developmental bibliotherapy, you are encouraged to connect instructional objectives in this area with writing topics and activities that allow advanced students to continue their exploration of the topics introduced through the process.

You can see that in developmental bibliography the ideal thinking and feeling path for the student is one from identification/connection, to relating emotionally to the feelings of the book characters, and finally to gaining new insight into ways to deal with a personal issue or experience. Because this is not a therapeutic or counseling situation, you should not assume that these stages must be reached, nor that you are responsible for moving the student along this path. It is sufficient to choose to use a selected novel in support of some of the typical issues of your advanced readers. Remember that for students expressing deep problems or concerns you will, of course, refer this to parents, counselors, and/or administrators as appropriate. The positive results of developmental bibliotherapy are worth your efforts.

NOVELS FOR BIBLIOTHERAPY LIST

The following list provides examples of novels suitable for developmental bibliotherapy. Remember to read the book first and use your good judgment in selecting a particular novel for a particular individual or group. Some books listed may contain mature themes, coarse language, and/or controversial topics.

+ ***The Giver* by Lois Lowry (1993):** *Focus: Identity, sense of fairness and justice.* In his Utopian world, Jonas has come to a crossroads in his life. Living in a perfect world where there is no fear or pain, Jonas begins to feel new emotions. He is about to receive his life's work assignment at the Ceremony of Twelve. Sharing his concerns with his family, he is reassured that the Committee of Elders will take care of him. What happened at the ceremony? Why was Jonas singled out? And what was the significance of the changing apple?

+ *Here's To You, Rachel Robinson* **by Judy Blume (1993):** *Focus: Perfectionism, expectations.* Rachel's perfect world becomes disrupted when her brother is expelled from boarding school and her sister has other problems. As the perfect student, sibling, and friend, Rachel puts pressure on herself to be the best at school and solve everyone's problems at home. How can she deal with all this pressure? Is there more to life than being perfect?

+ *Divergent* **by Veronica Roth (2011):** *Focus: Identity, family relationships.* In a dystopian world, Beatrice must choose between staying with her family or leaving to be her true self. It will soon be time for her decision as all 16-year-olds must choose one of five factions to belong to for the rest of their lives.

+ *If I Love You, Am I Trapped Forever?* **by M. E. Kerr (1973):** *Focus: Expectations, multipotentiality, perfectionism.* Being talented at many things can be a burden when the pressure is there from your parents and friends. And then Duncan Stein, a new student at Alan's school is suddenly challenging him as the "number one" golden boy at Cayuta High.

+ *The Facts and Fictions of Minna Pratt* **by Patricia MacLachlan (1988):** *Focus: Search for identity, family dynamics, creativity and musical talent.* Living in a family full of gifted and somewhat eccentric people, Mina is a serious student and a top-notch musician. She feels frustrated because her cello playing is not up to her standards, and her home is not the peaceful and orderly place she wishes it would be. Lucas, a new member of Minna's chamber music group, helps her to see her family and herself in a new light.

+ *Millicent Min, Girl Genius* **by Lisa Yee (2003):** *Focus: Making friends, social issues, acceleration, gender and intelligence issues.* It is summer and 11-year-old Millie is enrolled in a summer poetry class at college but not having much fun. Highly gifted, Millie will complete high school next year, so kids her age are jealous and her schoolmates feel about the same. What's worse, Millie's parents have arranged for her to tutor Stanford Wong, the geek. Enter Emily, a girl who amazingly doesn't know about Millie's exceptional intelligence. She seems to like Millie just for being herself. Can this friendship last? What will Millie have to do to keep her secret? Should she?

+ *Catalyst* **by Laurie Halse Anderson (2002):** *Focus: Multipotentiality, perfectionism.* Kate's life is full of excellence. She is an outstanding student and athlete. In spite of the loss of her mother several years earlier, Kate is in control. She is organized and logical and, living with her widowed father, a minister, she is sure her dream of attending MIT is well within reach. A sudden cluster of events changes everything. Her neighbors' house burns down and her father welcomes the family into Kate's home. Now Kate has to share her room and her home with Teri and her little brother. When a rejection letter arrives Kate realizes how her life is getting out of control. Can anything else possibly go wrong?

+ ***The Curious Incident of the Dog in the Night-Time* by Mark Haddon (2003):** *Focus: Twice exceptionality.* Christopher is an interesting sort of fellow. He finds comfort and relaxation in developing certain rules for his everyday life and solving math problems in his head. The stimulation of his surroundings are too much for his mind, so he creates patterns to control the chaos ("4 yellow cars in a row made it a Black Day, which is a day when I don't speak to anyone . . . "). Seeming a little odd to his neighbors, he is accused of killing his neighbor's poodle. Being the innocent victim of this accusation, Christopher decides to solve the mystery of the dog's death, hunting the killer in imitation of Sherlock Holmes. Relying on his abilities to confront things through logical deductions, his hunt for the killer forces him to interact with the complex social world around him and in the process discover more about himself, his family, and his own place in the world.

+ ***Walk Two Moons* by Sharon Creech (1994):** *Focus: Family relationships, friendship, cultural identity.* Thirteen-year-old Salamanca Tree Hiddle (Sal) travels from Ohio to Idaho to trace the steps of her mother who is missing. Accompanied by her eccentric grandparents, Sal entertains them with anecdotes about her friend, Phoebe, who told Sal an outrageous story about her mother vanishing, her encounter with lunatics, and the strange messages she supposedly received. Along the journey another story unfolds, that of Sal's strong desire to be reunited with her own mother and the importance of her Native American heritage.

+ ***Ironman* by Chris Crutcher (1995):** *Focus: Identity, family relationships, friendships, athletic talent.* Bo is angry. He seems to continually clash with those in authority, including his own father, his football coach, and his English teacher. Finding a way out of his frustrations, he gains new insights from his unlikely relationship with a TV personality, his reflection on the attitudes of his fellow anger-management group at school, and his own determination to be a triathlete.

+ ***Very Far Away From Anywhere Else* by Ursula K. Le Guin (1976):** *Focus: Social relationships, musical talent, multipotentiality.* This is the story of Owen and Natalie, friends and seniors in high school with two different frames of mind for their future. Somewhat of a misfit, Owen thinks he wants to be a scientist, but is not exactly sure what that means for him. Natalie, a musician, knows exactly what she wants and is determined to create and follow her own path. Owen's doubts and fears and his deep struggle to move forward purposefully into life are in sharp contrast with the shallow and self-absorbed actions of his male peers.

+ ***Counting by 7s* by Holly Goldberg Sloan (2013):** *Focus: Extreme giftedness, social relationships, friendship.* Willow, a 12-year-old genius, is obsessed with the number 7, her garden, and diagnosing medical conditions. She is hoping her start at a new school will help her to fit in and find friends. With the tragic death of her adoptive parents in a car crash, Willow loses her connections to the real world and must start over again. Through this tragedy, Willow finds herself in a new home and a new life with a new family and an unlikely cast of characters who are themselves putting down new roots.

+ ***Among Friends* by Caroline B. Cooney (1987):** *Focus: Social relationships.* Sometimes friendships are complicated. Jennie and her two friends seem to be drifting apart as Jennie is more and more seen at school as the star while Emily and Hillary become more jealous and resentful. Jennie and her friends must explore the question, "What is the price of success?"

+ ***No and Me* by Delphine de Viga (2007):** *Focus: Introversion, social justice, social relationships.* Lou is highly gifted (160 IQ), but painfully shy. When her teacher assigns a class project, Lou decides to follow the journey of a homeless girl. When her teacher endorses this project, shy Lou is pressured to follow through. At a train station she meets No, an 18-year-old homeless girl who quickly becomes her friend. Lou convinces her parents to allow No to live with them in spite of the fact that their home is overshadowed by the recent death of their baby and Lou's mother's reactive depression. Lou's class experiment results in changes for her, but not always in expected ways.

+ ***Jacob Have I Loved* by Katherine Paterson (1980):** *Focus: Family relationships, identity.* Louise is convinced that her sister Caroline is the golden girl in the family. She perceives Caroline as the receiver of all of the family's attention and encouragement while she was robbed. As she becomes a young woman, she begins to recognize the possibilities in her life apart from Caroline's. Emerging from the shadows, Louise comes to find independence and strength far beyond her childhood dreams.

Chapter 14

Technology, Students, and Novels
A Powerful Combination

How many books can a student in your class carry in his backpack? 5? 10? Oh, depends on the size? I know, trick question. It actually depends on the size of the storage device. Flash drive? Cloud? The sky is the limit! It is time to think in different ways about what students read, how they read it, and how they retrieve, share, and reflect on their reading.

For those of you saying, "Just tell me which books to get and how to use them in my reading program," you can skip this chapter. Just recognize that electronic media are deeply ingrained in your students' lives. For those of you already on the E-train or ready to get on board, read on.

Whether reading from a book or on an electronic device, reading is the same, or is it? Consider the multiple options available to today's reader. How about you? How many of these can you check off as personal experiences?

+ Got a print book from the library, a friend, or a local store.
+ Purchased a printed book online.
+ Purchased an eBook online.
+ Borrowed an eBook from the library or a friend.
+ Listened to an audio version of a book.
+ Stored a book in your cloud, computer, tablet, or eReader.
+ Read a book electronically.
+ Read an online book review.
+ Was influenced by an online book review.
+ Wrote an online book review.
+ Used social media to share a book.
+ Read a blog about books.
+ Joined a face-to-face book club.
+ Joined an online book discussion group.
+ Experienced an interactive novel.

Now think back 10 years. How many of those options were available? We know that modern literacy practices are changing. Recent research by the Pew Research Center (Desilver, 2014) indicates that reading books in general remains strong. Sixty-nine percent of Americans said they had read at least one book during the past year and the median number of books read was five. What is changing is the format people choose for their reading. Twenty-eight percent of those surveyed said they had read an eBook this past year. Among readers under 30, almost half read an eBook in the past year—twice as many eBook readers as were reported 3 years ago. The survey did not interview those under 18. How do you think your students would respond? In spite of the fact that large numbers of adults are reading eBooks, the number of printed copies read has not diminished. People are actually reading more!

In this chapter, you will learn about four areas of your reading program that can be enhanced through electronic media: accessing book recommendations and books, reading books, responding to and sharing the reading, and reflecting on what was read.

Technology is something that all current students have experienced from a very young age. As a result, they interact with the world and with technology in ways different from those who grew up without it. They also learn and engage differently, with electronic media complementing their learning. As a result, modern literacy practices are changing.

Technology, when used correctly, can increase student engagement and open new avenues of learning. If you choose to use technology in your classroom, you must first determine your anticipated student outcomes and how technology can support those outcomes. Technology does not automatically make a lesson or activity better, but, if used correctly, it can net amazing results.

ACCESSING BOOKS

Recommendations

In earlier chapters, you discovered book lists for the various genres of novels, including graphic novels, and for developmental bibliotherapy. Although these lists are a great start on selecting more advanced novels for your students, they are not enough. The vast majority of people choose books by asking for recommendations from friends or reading reviews, sometimes a combination of both. Your students may suggest books or you may want to select from the latest releases. You may be looking for a particular author, topic, or style of writing. Accessing good information on young adult novels has been made quite easy because of the electronic profiles available to you as well as those your students can create.

+ **Publishers and online retailers:** Going to a publisher's website will enable you to preview new releases as well as just-released books. Publishers and online retailers such as Amazon and Barnes & Noble often provide a peek inside the book with search options as well as additional information including reviews, interviews with authors, and even audio clips. You can readily see the availability of each book in multiple formats.

+ **Young Adult Library Services Association (YALSA; http://www.ala. org/yalsa/booklistsawards/booklistsbook):** This group is a division of the American Library Association. Here you can find YALSA's Book Awards and Selected Booklists.

+ **Goodreads (https://www.goodreads.com):** A free website for book lovers is available at Goodreads. You can read reviews and find lists of books by topic, genre, and recommended age. You can find lists of the "Best of (Year) Books for Young Adults" and other ages. You can also post reviews and keep an online list of what you have read, are now reading, and what you plan to read. You can join a discussion group, start a book club, connect with an author, or post your original writing. This website also includes an Indies section, particularly popular with young adults. Indies are small press and self-published books that can be downloaded onto eReaders. Other young adults are frequently sharing their thoughts on the most popular books of the moment as well as reviews, both negative and positive. These reviews can be good models for your own students' reviews.

+ **Young Adult Book Central (http://www.yabookscentral.com):** This young adult book community is the place for young adults to get information on the latest releases, including opportunities to review new books and win copies. You might want to join the community and allow members of your class to take turns reading recommended book lists, writing reviews, or reading the latest blogs. Also available on Facebook and Twitter.

+ **Student reviews:** You can use technology to engage your students in creating reviews and looking for recommendations from their peers. Google Forms (accessible through Google Drive) is an easy way for students to input information on books they have read. On a simple form, students can enter the title, author, genre, a "star" rating, and even offer a short summary. Once submitted, the data will be automatically compiled into a spreadsheet. Students can access that spreadsheet to look for books they want to read based on ratings and commentary from their peers. This can lead to a lot of impromptu conversations about books in and outside of the classroom.

Electronic Retrieval

How can your students access novels to read? For all practical purposes, students can retrieve novels through the printed page, eBooks, or audio books. Your students will likely use all of these. You can create a classroom e-library fairly easily and predownload books to a particular device accessible to your students. More and more options for free books as well as books loaned electronically are becoming available. Talk to your media specialist/librarian about what retrieval options are available at your school.

Electronic books. Electronic books are also known as eBooks. These electronic texts are available in multiple ways. They can be purchased online, accessed through a library-sponsored service, or downloaded from an Internet site such as http://read.gov. All require software to read the text and all require a reading device, which can be a computer, a tablet, an eReader, or a smartphone. EBooks may include hypermedia, links to text, data, graphics, audio, or video. They can be searched and the font size can be changed for ease of viewing. They may also include embedded references, details, and author notes. Electronic translations to multiple languages are also possible.

Sources for eBooks include:

+ **Guttenberg (https://www.gutenberg.org):** This is a digital library of free eBooks including many classics as well as subject categories by genre such as mystery fiction, science fiction, fantasy, contemporary fiction, and historical fiction. Look here for the Sherlock Holmes books as well as 49,000 free eBooks you can use in novel studies. Most of the books are also available as Kindle books.

+ **The National Archive (https://blog.archive.org/2014/02/21/popular-book-subjects):** This web address is an easy entre into the national archive of books, a nonprofit organization dedicated to making public access to books easy. Many classic works are available, such as all of Jane Austen's books. This website is definitely worth a peek.

+ **The Library of Congress (http://read.gov):** This Library of Congress sponsored website offers free reading of many American classics as well as a host of other reading materials such as the books that shaped America. The website also includes interviews with noted authors.

+ **Your school and local libraries:** Most libraries now have multiple service options for downloading and reading eBooks.

Audiobooks. These books were originally called books on tape. They are professionally recorded versions of novels available in CD or MP3 format, requiring either a CD player or an audio MP3 player. Audiobooks may be purchased or borrowed from the library in CD versions or download or streamed electronically, again for purchase or borrowing from the library. Like eBooks, most libraries now have extensive collections of audiobooks available online.

Sources for audiobooks include:

+ **Kids Learn Out Loud (http://kids.learnoutloud.com):** This is a website containing not only audiobooks but also videos and podcasts directed at children, including teens. The website has downloadable books and resources, all free, but also contains a selection of audiobooks for purchase.

+ **Audible.com:** Amazon's audible book service includes the first 30 days of use for free. The subscription rate is then $14.95 per month. This wide selection of books for children and young adults includes contemporary and classic literature as well as poetry and nonfiction.

+ **Loyal Books (formerly known as Books Should Be Free; http://www. loyalbooks.com):** This is a resource containing not only audiobooks, but eBook versions of books that are within the public domain. They have a children's section that includes classics appropriate for young adults.

+ **Lightspeed (http://www.lightspeedmagazine.com):** This is an online science fiction and fantasy magazine that has won several awards. Each month a new issue containing stories, interviews, and more can be viewed online or purchased for download. Not everything on this site is child or young adult friendly, so some previewing is required.

+ **Librophile (http://www.librophile.com/#!/audiobooks/popular/free):** This is an online library of books in both eBook and audiobook format. The site contains both free books and those available for purchase. The books, which number more than 100,000, are searchable by genre, or can be displayed in order of popularity or latest available.

+ **Other services:** Many services such as Amazon and Apple also carry audiobook versions. Amazon's audiobook versions can be purchased and downloaded through the Kindle store. Similarly iTunes has a large selection of audiobooks available for purchase and download.

RESPONDING TO AND SHARING READING

Selecting ways for students to respond to reading and share with others has changed significantly through the use of electronic media. Once students begin reading, whether printed books or electronic books, they are reacting to books, whether they realize it or not. Technology can easily be used to create a platform for students to talk about books.

Student Blogs

One of the simplest ways for you to create a place for discussion is to provide your students with book blogs. Many websites that host blogs are available, including WordPress. Commercial sites allow for blogs to be password protected, limiting who can see and interact with students posts. Blackboard, as well as many other learning platforms used in schools, has a blog function that you can access for book sharing. You can create a mock blog using Google Docs, where students can share with others in their group or class through the edit function and/or the comment section. A word on management when using Google Apps with groups of students in the same document: It can be helpful to have students each choose a font and color to do all of their own work in. Having students declare this in the very beginning of the document can make it easy for everyone to see who made which comments at a glance. This lends clarity to a document that can be managed well.

Blogs can be set up in several formats. Students can have their own individual book blogs, groups can share blogs, or there can be one blog shared by all students in a class. Blog topics can be chosen by the teacher or the students. When starting book blogs initially, it can be beneficial to choose topics or prompts for students to work from, particularly if students are new to discussing books. For example, you can direct students to complete blog entries on Novel Approach questions of the week in preparation for a group discussion. Responsibility can be gradually released, allowing options and eventually free choice once students are comfortable with discussion and the format.

Care should be taken to set up expectations not only for the blog itself but also for what comments and the resulting discussion should look like. Students are not always sure how to interact in school using technology. They need to be clear about what "appropriate and acceptable" looks like for a class assignment. Teaching students how to use an online sharing or discussion tool is important no matter how seemingly tech savvy they are. Eventually students will gain a comfort and rhythm, but only with time and experience. Teachers should be active participants, blogging about books and commenting as well.

Book Trailers

Another use of technology that students enjoy to "hook" someone into a book is creating a book trailer. Students are bombarded with movie trailers on television and the Internet. They know how much interest, hype, and discussion they can generate for movies. Many applications, including iMovie and Photostory can be used to create similar trailers for books. Students can tease potential readers with enough information to create interest and then leave the audience hanging, wanting to read the book in question. Students can create live-action trailers or simply a series of slides with an interesting voiceover and music. The process lends itself to both extremely tech-savvy students and those learning to work with new applications for the first time. It generates a buzz and excitement about reading and books and captures the creativity of students.

Online Discussion Circles

Using the pattern of the Novel Approach, conducting discussion groups online presents some challenges but none that cannot be overcome. Technology has opened a new world to students in this arena. Applications such as Skype, Facetime, and Google Hangouts allow students to video chat with one another, even with multiple users or groups. This allows for the same face-to-face feeling, and real-time interaction in which students explore their own reactions and perspectives. Students connect with one another on a level they might not otherwise achieve. In many of these applications, students can screenshare, a process by which they can show images on their computers, including pictures, videos, writings, or other media without having to be physically present.

This technology can be used to pair individual students in other schools, states, or even countries. It allows for "buddy" classes where students with different backgrounds and experiences can find common ground around books and see things from other perspectives. Schools can even partner with other schools. The world becomes a much smaller and more accessible place when technology like this is used. It creates an excitement about reading and a deeper understanding of how people connect to books.

Of course, if your students are able to engage in a face-to-face discussion, they will reap many rewards unavailable online. The tone of voice, the facial expressions, and the patterns of listening and interacting are not the same online as in person. However, there may be times when online discussions are merited and, in fact, a good option. Using online live discussion is preferred over discussion forums or blogs so that students get the opportunity to listen, reflect, connect, and respond in an immediate fashion. You may want to connect with a group unavailable to you, such as students at another school or in a different state or country. You may use the option to connect with homebound students or others who are unable to be physically present. You may choose to add special guests to your discussion group such as an author, librarian, school administrator, or someone else who has read the book and would add to the discussion. In those cases, you can use a combination of live and online presence for participants. Always remember the goal of using technology to enhance the discussion and add inclusiveness rather than using it just for the sake of adding technology. Another option that may support your learning goals is to use a video recording tool to record all or part of a discussion circle for later student analysis, looking for ways to improve discussion skills. Students are effective critics of their discussions when they are reminded of the criteria for good discussions.

Online book clubs are available at several sites for young adults including http:// www.goodreads.com. Preview a site by joining yourself and participating prior to making any recommendations to students or using in class. Other online book clubs are possible as you connect with other teachers and choose a format and discussion guidelines prior to connecting your classes. Partnering with another teacher who uses the Novel Approach enables you to have a common language and process for guiding the online discussions.

Another relatively easy way to conduct online discussion circles that do not rely on live online connections is to use Google Docs or an online discussion forum (similar to the process of using this platform for blogging). A guiding question is posed by the group leader and other members of the small group are responsible for submitting comments and reaction to other's comments. Because this is asynchronous (not everyone at once) it allows for "discussion" without planning a particular time for a meeting. You would assign a time period within which the discussion was open and then closed for postings. Following the online discussion, you can direct the leader to summarize the students' reactions to the reading and comments on assigned questions, posting it as the final forum entry. Guide the students on how to post, how to connect to other's comments, and how to give reasons for their thinking as they comment online.

Reflecting on Reading

Activities using electronic media can unlock creativity and critical thinking in students and garner interesting reflections. Many of the suggested learning activities presented in Chapter 6 can be adapted to use electronic media. For example, ask your students to write blog entries as if they were a particular character in the novel. Taking on the role of a novel's character and looking at things from an alternative perspective is an exercise in critical and creative thinking that is not only beneficial for students but is also engaging. Other students can respond and continue discussion while in character. A more difficult variation is to write a blog from the perspective of a place in a novel. The possibilities are limited only by the imagination of the student and teacher. It requires almost no technological changes to create these variations and the variations can be differentiated for each student. There are many options in the creative vein, particularly when talking about writing from a character's perspective or portraying a person or place from a novel.

Social Media

Students today are intimately familiar with social media and one simply has to do a web search to find Facebook and Twitter feeds written as if they belonged to fictional characters. Facebook feeds, like blogging, can replace the fairly common assignment of journaling in the persona of a specific character. You can assign a more focused entry such as sharing the feelings or actions of a character in response to an event, guiding students to reveal their true understanding of character traits. Twitter, with its character limit, also asks students to condense a great deal of information and insight into a much smaller space, requiring students to carefully focus on word choice.

Twitter feeds can also be an incredibly interesting way of summarizing stories. Students must think carefully about the most important message, person, or event in a novel. You can ask students to tweet the essential theme of their novel or a short message summarizing a book review. The character limit can also lend itself to quoting "sound bites" from books to spark interest and discussion. This is another area where creativity can open a world of possibilities and allow students to shine.

Twitter and Facebook-like feeds can spark discussion, but are somewhat limited in capacity. However there are myriad ways to start deep and lasting conversations and student interactions revolving around books. Google Apps is one of the most versatile options in this vein. Using Google Apps, students can create documents, spreadsheets, quizzes, surveys, slideshows, and much more. They can create these alone, with partners, or in groups. Students can share their work with others to edit (good for partner and group projects), or just to share and comment.

Another option for reflecting and sharing online is Pinterest, where you can invite the novel group to develop a Pinterest page for their particular novel. Ask them to pin any relevant content or direct specific items to be added, like history of dragons in literature.

For bringing out the creativity in your students, try Make Beliefs Comix (http://www.makebeliefscomix.com). Using this tool, you can ask students to create a graphic of one section of the novel in cartoon form. Shift their thinking by asking, "If this were a graphic novel, how would this event be depicted?" Using media familiar to your students, you can ask them to text or chat. At the beginning or end of a novel discussion, ask students to partner with someone outside the group to convey some brief comment on the story as it stands at the end of this section of reading. Encourage sharing with parents. Sharing thoughts with authors is also a great way to keep students thinking about reading and writing. Invite students to search for a website for the author of their novel and write a brief letter to the author.

SUMMARY OF ELECTRONIC RESOURCES

The following list includes electronic tools you may access to develop or adapt creative and critical thinking skills for student response to novel readings. In addition to these electronic options, you will find hundreds of apps and online programs to enrich and extend the Novel Approach.

+ **Facebook (http://www.facebook.com):** Facebook is a social media website on which users set up their own profiles. People "friend" each other and can see and comment on one another's status updates. This website continuously evolves and allows users to share websites, articles, photos, videos and more in addition to their own thoughts, known as status updates.

+ **Facetime:** Facetime is an Apple application that comes loaded on most new Apple products including iPads and iPhones. This technology allows users to video chat in real time, forging a deeper connection than a simple phone call.

+ **Glogster (http://glogster.edu):** This site can be used to create an online book poster that acts as an advertisement for the book students just read. Students should include the title and author of the book and key characters, use pictures that support the storyline, and create a tagline that will make others want to read the book.

+ **Google Hangouts (accessible via Google+ in Google Apps; http://www.apps.google.com):** Google Plus is a social media website that organizes users into circles. However, one of the most interesting features is Google Hangouts, which is a video conferencing application within Google Plus. This allows users to video chat, share screens, and even easily have large group chats or virtual classes. No additional software is required, as this is a web-hosted application.

+ **Google Apps (http://www.apps.google.com):** Google Apps is a series of applications run by Google. Anyone with a Gmail (Google Mail) e-mail address has access to a Google Drive—a cloud storage space. Many school districts have worked with Google to create Google Accounts for their students that exist within a walled garden, which limits who the students may interact with. These applications include Google Documents, Spreadsheets, and Slides, which function like Microsoft Word, Excel, and PowerPoint respectively. There are also Google Sites, Plus, and Hangouts, which allow technologically savvy users to interact with others on more levels. All things created with Google Apps are shareable, which allows the user to not only show other people documents, but invite them to edit and/or comment in real time, allowing for truly deep collaboration.

+ **Go Teen Writers (http://goteenwriters.blogspot.com):** This blog spot offers encouragement and a community for teen writers.

+ **Letters About Literature (http://read.gov/letters):** At this webpage, you can find our more on Letters About Literature, a national contest in which students in grades 4–12 write letters to favorite authors telling how the author's book has affected their lives. There is an annual award and national recognition for several letter writers as well as their libraries.

+ **Photostory (http://microsoft-photo-story.en.softonic.com):** Microsoft Photostory (similar newer applications include Windows Moviemaker which can be accessed by the same link) is a presentation software that turns still images into a movie. Users can add narration and music for a truly multimedia presentation.

+ **Shelfari (http://www.shelfari.com):** Shelfari is a community-powered encyclopedia for book lovers. Create a virtual bookshelf, discover new books, connect with friends and learn more about your favorite books—all for free.

+ **Skype (http://www.skype.com):** Skype is free downloadable software that allows users to make online phone calls and video calls. The application also allows screen-sharing, a way to show the other parties in the call what is on your computer screen. This allows students to interact with other individuals and groups they cannot travel to see and has a great deal of versatility.

+ **Twitter (http://www.twitter.com):** Twitter is another social media outlet. Users "tweet" updates that are limited to 140 characters. These tweets update in real time, allowing for virtual "conversations," and have become a way to discover breaking news. The limited number of characters adds an interesting dynamic to social media.

References

Anderson, L. W., & Krathwohl, D. R. (Eds.). (2001). *A taxonomy for learning, teaching, and assessing: A revision of Bloom's taxonomy of educational objectives.* Boston, MA: Allyn & Bacon.

A practical school for girls. (1877, March 1). *Godey's Lady's Book.* Retrieved from http://www.accessible-archives.com/2014/03/godeys-says-america-needs-practical-schools-girls/#ixzz3cmvNU0Yv

Cotton, K. (1995). *School improvement research series close up #5: Classroom questioning.* Northwest Regional Educational Laboratory. Retrieved from http://www.nwrel.org/scpd/sirs/3/cu5.html

Desilver, D. (2014, January 21). Overall book readership stable, but e-books becoming more popular. *Pew Research Center.* Retrieved from http://www.pewresearch.org/fact-tank/2014/01/21/overall-book-readership-stable-but-e-books-becoming-more-popul

Kingore, B. L (2004). *Differentiation: Simplified, realistic, and effective.* Austin, TX: Professional Associates.

Liparulo, R. (2010, June 3). 5 elements that make fantasy fiction feel real. *Novel Rocket.* Retrieved from http://www.novelrocket.com/2010/06/5-elements-that-make-fantasy-fiction.html

McGuffy's fifth eclectic reader. (1879). New York, NY: American Book Company.

Twain, M. (1885). *The adventures of Huckleberry Finn.* Retrieved from http://www.gutenberg.org/cache/epub/76/pg76.txt

About the Author

Janice I. Robbins, Ph.D., is an adjunct professor in gifted education at William & Mary and at Rutgers University. She was formerly Curriculum Chief for the Department of Defense Schools worldwide as well as the Fairfax County, VA, district coordinator of gifted programs, a school principal, and a resource teacher in gifted education.